hristian PERFECTION

Also by J. R. Zurcher:

Touched With Our Feelings

Visit us at www.reviewandherald.com
for information on other Review and Herald products.

To order, call 1-800-765-6955.

What Inspiration Has to Say About

Christian PERFECTION

by **J. R. Zurcher**

Translated by Edward E. White

REVIEW AND HERALD® PUBLISHING ASSOCIATION
HAGERSTOWN MD 21740

The author assumes full responsibility for the accuracy
of all facts and quotations as cited in this book.

Unless otherwise noted, Bible texts in this book are from the
Holy Bible, New International Version. Copyright © 1973, 1978,
1984, International Bible Society. Used by permission of
Zondervan Bible Publishers.

This book was
Edited by Gerald Wheeler
Copyedited by Lori Halvorsen and James Cavil
Designed by Saschane Stephenson
Electronic makeup by Shirley M. Bolivar
Cover art by Photo Disc
Typeset: 10/14 Bookman Old Style

PRINTED IN U.S.A.

06 05 04 03 02   5 4 3 2 1

R&H Cataloging Service
Zurcher, Jean Rudolf, 1918-
    Christian perfection. Translated by Edward E. White.

    1. Perfection–Religious aspects–Seventh-day Adventists.
I. White, Edward E., trans. II. Title.

234.8

The original edition in French, *La Perfection Chrétienne,* was published by
the Editions "Belle Rivière," Lausanne, Switzerland, in 1994.

ISBN: 0-8280-1588-0

DEDICATION

To Anna, my beloved wife;
whose piety and meek and quiet
spirit have greatly contributed to
the perfecting of my own spiritual life.

ACKNOWLEDGMENTS

My special thanks for the help received from my friend Edward E. White, who translated the original French publication. My thanks also to Frederic and Drusilla Zurcher as well as Cari Beringham for their greatly appreciated contribution to the finishing touches in preparation for the English edition.

Key to Abbreviations
of E. G. White Book Titles

CONTENTS

PREFACE

Christian perfection has always been the subject of heated discussions, for all Christians do not grant the same value to the concept. The majority consider it as a moral ideal that only Jesus Christ has ever been able to achieve. Others believe that perfection constitutes the central aim of Christian living, a goal toward which all Christians should strive. For still others perfection is such a fundamental and absolute necessity that they can see no hope for salvation without it.

Clearly under the influence of the Greek philosophy, which confers an absolute meaning to the idea of perfection, some Church Fathers considered that God alone could be perfect. Consequently, according to them, perfection was probably beyond human reach. At best, they thought that apart from the person of Jesus Himself, only a few choice individuals may have attained it—namely, those whom the church calls "saints."

In contrast, the Reformers taught that perfection should be a concern to all believers, although no one should ever claim to have achieved it. "Perfectionist" tendencies influenced nearly all the revival movements springing from the Reformation. Not content just to assert that Christian perfection demanded a moral lifestyle free from sin, supporters of perfectionism have sometimes claimed that it also implied the restoration of human nature—that is to say, one from which the power of sin would have been expunged.

In the 1960s, for example, many Seventh-day Adventists found themselves troubled by the teaching of an extremist group that affirmed that Christian perfection demanded not only victory over sin, but also that "the sinful human nature should be eradicated from the heart and spirit," and "the corrupt and carnal nature destroyed and not merely neutralized." Such a teaching aroused a strong and active reaction. Numerous articles, pamphlets, and books appeared on the subject of perfection, seeking to denounce errors in the interpretation of Bible verses and, more specifically, of certain extracts from the pen of Ellen G. White.

This presentation does not intend to retrace the history of the various theories that have challenged each other throughout the centuries. That would be an exercise in futility for those who wish to know what the Bible teaches on the subject of Christian perfection. Nor is it a treatise in systematic theology with commentaries and references to the many authors who have dealt with the subject. On the contrary, we have deliberately chosen to keep closely to the Bible, hoping above all to place the reader in direct contact with the Sacred Word. It should not surprise the reader that I have extensively quoted biblical passages.

Also, I cite Ellen G. White's comments on Christian perfection. Among all the authors who have dealt with this subject, no one, to my knowledge, has kept so faithfully to the spirit of the Bible.

It is indeed vital for us to understand that God calls all believers to perfection. However, some have given the word a meaning totally foreign to the biblical idea, leading to theological aberrations. We hope that this book will not only correct such misunderstandings, but also kindle a spiritual revival in each individual reader.

P Christian ERFECTION

CHAPTER ONE

AN APPEAL
TO
PERFECTION

No one can read Scripture without feeling a powerful call to an ideal beyond unaided human reach. In fact, the entire Bible summons us to live in a way whose value is more than the number of years granted to us, but a level of moral and spiritual perfection whose model is Jesus Christ Himself.

Every Christian is aware of God's command to Abraham, the father of the faithful, to "walk before me, and be thou perfect" (Gen.17:1, KJV). Moreover, Jesus proclaimed as He was concluding his comments on the law: "Be perfect, therefore, as your heavenly Father is perfect" (Matt. 5:48).

Perfection is therefore precisely the goal toward which we expect every disciple of Jesus to aim. The apostle Paul made it the prime objective of his life. Indeed, he writes, "Not that I have already obtained all this, or have already been made *perfect, but* I press on to take hold of that for which Christ Jesus took hold of me. Brothers, I do not consider myself yet to have taken hold of it. But one thing I do: Forgetting what is behind and straining toward what is ahead, I press on toward the goal to win the prize for which God had called heavenward in Christ Jesus" (Phil. 3:12-14). Then, addressing his readers, he adds: "Join with others in following my example, brothers, and take note of those who live according to the pattern we gave you" (verse 17).

Likewise, James, in his Epistle, exhorts the scattered Christians to persevere in trials in order to arrive at perfection: "Consider it pure joy, my brothers, whenever you face trials of many kinds, because you know that the testing of your faith develops perseverance. Perseverance must finish its work so that you may be *mature and complete,* not lacking anything" (James 1:2-4).

1. Perfection, an innate need

If perfection were an impossibility, the sacred writers would not exhort us to seek it. God would not call believers to reach out for perfection if there did not exist within humanity a real need for it, inborn in human nature in a manner similar to the thought of eternity that God also purposefully set in the human heart (Eccl. 3:11). Likewise, our need for perfection does not manifest itself only in the spiritual life. It appears in every activity—in the arts, in sports, and every other endeavor. In reality, a quest for perfection has motivated all the great material and technological accomplishments of modern society. In the spiritual life it impels the believer to pursue moral values.

It would therefore be inconceivable that God would have created in humanity an urgent need for perfection without at the same time giving us the potential to accomplish it. If indeed Christian perfection were entirely unobtainable, it would be all the more incomprehensible that Jesus Himself would have pointed to it at all.

2. The biblical meaning of the word "perfect"

The real problem is not so much a matter of knowing whether perfection is possible or not as it is to determine how the Bible writers understood the word "perfect" and its derivatives.

Discovering what the biblical writers meant is never easy. All too often we read the Scriptures through our own preconceived ideas or according to what we ourselves intend to prove. It is difficult for us to be purely objective, to allow the Bible to speak for itself, or to listen attentively to what it tells us. And it becomes even more difficult when we do not know the precise meaning of words and expressions as used in other languages and cultures.

Often we approach passages about perfection with preconceived ideas. In addition, we interpret them in light of philosophical concepts foreign to the true spirit of the Bible. To further confuse the issue, we read the words of the Bible in the context of today's language instead of the meaning of the words at the time the biblical writers used them. As a result we make the Bible say not what it really intends, but what we ourselves think it means. No wonder the same verses, even the same words, sometimes provide the basis for the most contradictory doctrines!

To interpret biblical words and phrases properly, we must follow some basic rules. No matter what the topic, it goes without saying that we must capture the original meaning of the Hebrew or Greek words as used by Old and New Testament writers. Then, of course, it is essential to place the words in their proper context, not only in terms of their immediate context and the book of the Bible they form a part of, but also in the Bible as a whole.

Many words have more than one meaning, including the word "perfect" in the Bible. We can grasp their various nuances only by considering the context. That is why we must do our best to capture the meaning understood by the biblical writer. To do that, translators have had to resort to the use of expressions other than "perfect" or "perfection."

As we examine the different Bible translations we will be surprised at the scarcity of verses in which the Hebrew and Greek words have been translated into our modern languages by "perfect" or "perfection." The original text of both testaments has about 800 appearances of the word "perfect," only 100 of which have been translated by using the word "perfect." In the remaining cases translators have employed other expressions that render the general meaning of the specific passage.

For example, the original Hebrew states that the repairing of Solomon's Temple was "perfect," but modern translators have appropriately translated it by the word "finished" (2 Chron. 24:14). Likewise, in the New Testament scholars have rendered the Greek word *téleios* in a variety of ways, depending on the message of the verse. Speaking of the feast of the Passover that Jesus attended when he was 12 years old, the New International Version reads "after the Feast was over" (Luke 2:43). Another passage translates the word *perfect* by "reach my goal" (Luke 13:32), or again by the verbs "to finish" or "to complete" (John 4:34; 5:36; 19:28; Acts 20:24). In His priestly prayer Jesus says that He "finished" (John 17:4,

KJV), or "completed" (NIV), the work that God had given Him to do.

Obviously we will not study here all the Bible verses that use the words "perfect" or "perfection." Instead, we shall confine ourselves to those cases in which the words relate to God or humanity. We find that in such instances the Hebrew words *tâm* and *tâmîm* as well as *shalem* have generally been translated by expressions such as: "honest," "right," "accomplished," "good," "innocent," "peaceful," and a few others. Concerning humans specifically, the meaning contained in these words expresses "perfection," "fullness," "integrity," and "sincerity toward God."

Likewise the writers of the New Testament have given to the Greek *téleios* and its derivatives the same meanings. The word also carries the concept of something that is "perfect," "finished," which has "reached completeness," "reached its goal," or of that which "has come to maturity."

A detailed study of some typical examples first from the Old Testament and then from the New Testament will suffice to give us an understanding of the meaning intended by the biblical concept of perfection. To understand these expressions properly, we must recognize that perfection according to the Bible is the goal to which all Christians should aim.

CHAPTER TWO

GOD'S
PERFECTION

Surprising as it may be, only one passage in the whole Bible mentions God's perfection. In it Jesus exhorts all His disciples: "Be perfect, therefore, as your heavenly Father is perfect" (Matt. 5:48).

Of course, God is perfect in the most complete meaning of the word, but the sacred writers never needed to say so. Actually, placed in its context, the perfection to which Jesus had in mind does not refer directly to God Himself, but rather to His perfect and merciful relationships with humanity. The writers of the Old Testament never apply the idea of perfection to God's person in order to define Him. Rather they describe the perfection of His works, His ways, His laws, and His omniscience with the word *tâmîn,* that is to say "perfect."

In fact, only four passages in the Old Testament specifically apply the word "perfect" in relation to God. These four instances actually describe incidences in which God performs His perfect acts on behalf of humanity.

1. His works are perfect

In his magnificent song to the glory of God, Moses is the first to describe the perfect works of Him who led His people as a father does his children: "He is the Rock, his works are perfect, and all his ways are just. A faithful God who does no wrong, upright and just is he" (Deut. 32:4).

What works are they? It is important to note that if we wish to understand the meaning of the adjective, it is not a question here of God's created works. Certainly, as Paul writes: "For since the creation of the world God's invisible qualities—his eternal power and divine nature—have been clearly seen, being understood from what has been made." The apostle declares also that those who do not wish to see them are "without excuse" (Rom. 1:20).

Rather, the perfect works that Moses recalls in this long poem to God's glory are those the Lord wrought on Israel's behalf as He delivered it from Egypt and led it to the borders of Canaan. In contrast to Israel's continual rebellion, the great prophet shows that God had a perfect relationship between Himself and His people as He manifested patience, goodness, faithfulness, and justice. "He shielded him and cared for him; he guarded him as the apple of his eye" (Deut. 32:10).

We cannot emphasize enough that the perfection of God's works, as it applies to His children, is a matter of the perfect relationship that He maintains with His people despite their unfaithfulness to Him.

21

2. His ways are perfect

In the preceding verse Moses had already declared that "all his ways are just." David twice declares them perfect: "As for God, his way is perfect; the word of the Lord is flawless. He is a shield for all who take refuge in him" (2 Sam. 22:31; Ps. 18:30).

God's ways are not always easy to understand. Sometimes they seem strange. Often they even appear incomprehensible. Paul himself knew that very well: "How unsearchable his judgments, and his ways beyond tracing out!" (Rom. 11:33). Who can really grasp God's providential acts in the complex history of nations, in the mysterious fulfillment of the plan of salvation or simply in the smallest secrets of one's own personal life?

Yet thanks to the "flawless" word of the Lord the believer can discern the Lord's hand "in all your ways" (Prov. 3:6). By faith he recognizes that "in all things God works for the good of those who love him" (Rom. 8:28). Through personal experience, as with David, we can know that all God does expresses His mercy and seeks the happiness of all those who trust in Him.

3. His law is perfect

In the first part of Psalm 19 David considers the marvelous laws that govern our world. He is not unaware that "your laws endure to this day. . . . By them you have preserved my life" (Ps. 119:91-93). But beyond the unchangeable laws of nature the psalmist reveals his wonder at the moral law which he describes as perfect: "The law of the Lord is perfect, reviving the soul. The statutes of the Lord are trustworthy, making wise the simple" (Ps. 19:7).

For David the law of the Lord is the testimony of the eternal, that is to say, the very expression of God's character. The sign of His union with His people, He gave it to humanity to govern their relationship both with Himself and with our fellow neighbors, a relationship established on love. This law thus appeared perfect in David's sight. He seems at a loss for adjectives to describe it. Not only was it true, and all its commandments right, pure, and just, "more precious than gold," "sweeter than honey" (verse 10), but above all, "the law of the Lord is perfect," because of the effect it has on the one who puts it into practice, "reviving the soul," "making wise the simple" (verse 7). The law's instructions give "light to the eyes" and "joy to the heart" (verse 8). "In keeping them there is great reward" (verse 11).

Because the law of the Lord is perfect, it is indeed a law of love that governs the perfection of the relationships that should exist between human beings and God and between human beings themselves.

4. His knowledge is perfect

Contemplating God's omniscience, visible not only throughout the grandeur of the universe but also in terms of His relationship with humanity, should constantly awe us. "Do you know . . . those wonders of him who is perfect in knowledge?" Job asks (Job 37:16). "Can you probe the limits of the Almighty?" (Job 11:7). "Canst thou find out the Almighty unto perfection?" (verse 7, KJV).

David, confronted with the universe's immensity and humanity's smallness, declared: "When I consider your heavens, the work of your fingers, the moon and the stars, which you have set in place, what is man that you are mindful of him, the son of man that you care for him?" (Ps. 8:3, 4).

The psalmist faces a God who knows him to perfection.

23

The Lord, he says, can "perceive my thoughts from afar" (Ps. 139:2) and is "familiar with all my ways" (verse 3). He knows all things before they have happened and nothing escapes His notice. "Such knowledge is too wonderful for me, too lofty for me to attain" (verse 6) David concludes.

As he contemplated God's providential acts, whether manifested toward Israel or to the rest of mankind as He seeks to lead all to salvation, Paul found himself compelled to exclaim: "Oh, the depth of the riches of the wisdom and knowledge of God! How unsearchable his judgments, and his paths beyond tracing out! Who has known the mind of the Lord? Or who has been his counselor?" (Rom. 11:33, 34).

Conclusion

As we analyze these few texts, it is evident that they are speaking not of the perfection of God's divine nature, but rather of His acts on behalf of human salvation. As James reminds us: "Every good and perfect gift is from above, coming down from the Father of the heavenly lights, who does not change like shifting shadows" (James 1:17).

God's deeds are perfect because they are the outworking of His justice, His faithfulness, His uprightness, and His goodness. His ways are likewise perfect because they seek the good of all those who trust in Him. His law is also perfect because it is a law of love—a "law that gives freedom" (verse 25) and is designed for human restoration. Perfect as well is His knowledge of all things, for it contains all wisdom and knowledge.

To understand that God's perfection refers to His merciful relationships with His creation already constitutes an initial clarification of the biblical meaning of the concept of perfection. This relationship is the perfect expression of

God's character, and it is in this particular sense that Jesus exhorted Christians to "be perfect . . . as your heavenly Father is perfect" (Matt. 5:48). It is important to emphasize this point, because as we will discover in the following pages, human perfection dwells not within human nature, but in the substance of our relationship with God and with our neighbor.

CHAPTER THREE

Humanity's Perfection

I t is not our intention here to study all the Old Testament verses containing *tâmîm* and *shalem* and translated "perfect." Instead, we shall confine our analysis to individuals whom Scripture specifically states to have been perfect. The Bible has only a few examples.

1. Noah's perfect walk

Noah is the first person to whom the author of Genesis ascribes the adjective "perfect" *(tâmîm)*. "Noah was a just man and *perfect* in his generations, and Noah walked with God" (Gen. 6:9, KJV). Obviously it does not mean that Noah was a perfect individual in the sense that he was without sin or that he had reached a holy state in which one no longer sins. A later incident in his life shows us at least one of his faults, with unhappy consequences for his youngest son (Gen. 9:21-25).

The Bible considers Noah a righteous man because he maintained a just relationship with God. He was perfect because his integrity toward God was total. In any case, these qualities do not concern Noah himself, his human nature, but rather the way he "walked with God." In other words, the manner in which he lived his life in relation with God accorded with God's mission for him. For this reason Scripture counts Noah among the heroes of faith. For "by faith Noah, when warned about things not yet seen, in holy fear built an ark to save his family. By his faith he condemned the world and became heir of the righteousness that comes by faith" (Heb. 11:7).

2. Abraham's perfect faith

Genesis 17:1 employs *tâmîm*, the same word used to describe Noah's perfection, but a significant difference exists between Noah's walk and that of Abraham, as we see by the preposition that qualifies it. While Noah walked *"with God"* (Gen. 6:9), Abraham was commanded to walk *"before"* Him (Gen. 17:1), that is, in His presence and "before the eyes of him to whom we must give account" (Heb. 4:13).

Taken in its context, the divine command allows us to suppose that Abraham's life up to then had not been what it should. That is why God renewed His covenant at this time, exhorting Abraham from now on to walk in such a manner as—to use the words of Paul—"to win the prize for which God has called me heavenward" (Phil. 3:14).

Genesis specifies that God chose Abraham "so that he will direct his children and his household after him to keep the way of the Lord by doing what is right and just, so that the Lord will bring about for Abraham what he has promised him" (Gen. 18:19). The patriarch had to fulfill the conditions so that his posterity would "become a great and powerful nation, and all nations on earth will be blessed through him" (verse 18).

Most certainly, Abraham's life was not without mistakes, any more than was Noah's. The story of his life leaves no doubt about that. Yet at the end of the patriarch's life God could tell Isaac that "because Abraham obeyed me and kept my requirements, my commands, my decrees and my laws" (Gen. 26:5), "through your offspring all nations on earth will be blessed" (verse 4). Because Abraham maintained such a perfect relationship with God, "he was called God's friend" (James 2:23).

Scripture rightly considers Abraham to be "the father of all who believe" and "who also walk in the footsteps of the faith that our father Abraham had" (Rom. 4:11, 12). For Abraham's faith is really the model of the faith that "obeys" and "works" "expressing itself" (NIV), "justifies," and "saves," according to the definitions that the apostle Paul gave it (Rom. 1:5; Gal. 5:6; Rom. 3:22, 26; 4:3-5; Eph. 2:8).

Abraham believed "against all hope" (Rom. 4:18). His trust in God was complete. Although "living by faith," he still died "and did not receive the things promised." But he "saw them and welcomed them from a distance" (Heb. 11:13). "For he was looking forward to the city with foundations, whose architect and builder is God" (verse 10). Better than anyone else, Abraham is the example of the just who lived by faith, and whose "faith . . . by works . . . was made perfect" (James 2:22, KJV).

3. Job's perfect testimony

The Bible writes of Job, as it did of Noah, that he was

a man "perfect *[tāmîm]* and upright" (Job 1:1, KJV). Twice
God declared of him: "'There is none like him in the earth,
a perfect and upright man, one that feareth God, and es-
cheweth evil" (Job 1:8, KJV; 2:3, KJV).

That does not mean at all that Job was without sin,
any more than Noah or Abraham, although his friends
were unable to accuse him of any fault whatsoever. Job
himself did not claim to be righteous or innocent. On the
contrary, as he himself said: "If I justify myself, mine own
mouth shall condemn me: if I say, I am perfect, it shall
also prove me perverse" (Job 9:20, KJV).

The patriarch was aware that "there is no one righteous, not even one" (Rom. 3:10) and that "Jews and
Gentiles alike are all under sin" (verse 9). Even if Job felt
like Paul, who wrote "my conscience is clear, but that does
not make me innocent!" (1 Cor. 4:4), he still declared at
the conclusion of his painful experience, "I despise myself,
and repent in dust and ashes" (Job 42:6).

What then constitutes Job's perfection? As with Noah
and Abraham, it was his relationship with God, his integrity and uprightness before Him, his absolute confidence in God, and in particular, his steadfast faith toward
Him of whom he was to say after his trial: "My ears had
heard of you but now my eyes have seen you" (verse 5).

4. David's perfect heart

Even if we do not understand the biblical idea of perfection as a state of sinless perfection, it still surprises us
that the Bible presents King David as a model of perfection. All the more since we know that God did not regard
him as worthy to build the Temple in His honor, because
he had shed so much blood (1 Chron. 22:8).

Comparing the life of David with that of his successors,

the author of the book of 1 Kings declares twice that David's heart was perfect *(shalem)*. Speaking of Solomon he writes: "his heart was not perfect *[shalem],* with the Lord his God, as was the heart of David his father" (1 Kings 11:4, KJV). The biblical writer makes the same comment again when he also compares another descendant, King Abijam, with David (1 Kings 15:3).

It is important to notice here that the adjective "perfect" does not describe David the man as such, nor his life, but "his heart." When God explained His reason for choosing David to be the future king, he said to the prophet Samuel: "The Lord does not look at the things man looks at. Man looks at the outward appearance, but the Lord looks at the heart" (1 Sam. 16:7).

In biblical parlance the heart generally means the inner person, what is hidden within, the depth of an individual's being, the secret thoughts (1 Chron. 28:9). But in a more exact manner and in the majority of cases Scripture views the heart as the seat of the will, the "place" where a human being exercises the power of decision. For example, notice the following typical biblical expression: "I sought in mine heart" (Eccl. 2:3, KJV; 2 Cor. 9:7, KJV; 1 Cor. 7:37, KJV).

Thus when Samuel recalled the election of David ("the Lord has sought out a man after his own heart" [1 Sam. 13:14]), he meant that the choice of David was made in accordance with the will of God and according to the inner nature of the heart of David. God alone knows what a person is really like, what spiritual desires motivate him or her, such as sincerity, uprightness, integrity, a need for righteousness, a hunger for truth, and an absolute trust in God's goodness.

David not only possessed these exceptional spiritual

qualities to the highest degree, but he could express them beautifully in his many psalms. He could record with perfect artistry how each one profoundly affected him in his battle for right over wrong or operated in his search for God as he confronted life's various trials. For this reason believers of all ages have used the words of the psalms to express to God the sentiments of their own hearts.

It is precisely in this way that David stands out as a model of perfection despite his weaknesses and failures. Perhaps it was on the occasion of his most serious sin that he expressed most perfectly the sentiments that God accepts when a sinner confronts his or her sin. Whatever the enormity of one's sin, the sinner will find in Psalm 51 the most perfect model of repentance.

When faced with his own sin, David's repentance was perfect, just as was his submission to God's judgment. His request for forgiveness and his confidence in God's goodness were also both perfect. So too was his burning need for restoration: "Surely you desire truth in the inner parts; you teach me wisdom in the inmost place. . . . Create in me a pure heart, O God, and renew a steadfast spirit within me" (Ps. 51:6-10).

Contrary to then current religious practice, David understood that to reestablish the relationship with God that sin had broken, it was not enough to offer burnt offerings such as "thousands of rams" and "rivers of oil" (Micah 6:7). "You do not delight in sacrifice, or I would bring it," David proclaims. "You do not take pleasure in burnt offerings. The sacrifices of God are a broken spirit; a broken and contrite heart, O God, you will not despise" (Ps. 51:16, 17).

In his consecration prayer at Gibeon, Solomon forcefully summarized the reasons why his father David was a man after God's heart and why we could regard him as a model of perfection: "You have shown great kindness to your servant, my father David, because he was faithful to you and righteous and upright in heart" (1 Kings 3:6). Finally Asaph, singer and prophet of Israel, declared in Psalm 78:72: "And David shepherded them [the sheep of Israel] with integrity of heart." In other words, with a will in perfect submission to that of God's.

5. King Asa's perfect life

A final example of a person the Old Testament describes as having a perfect *(shalem)* heart throughout his whole life is King Asa, who reigned over Judah in Jerusalem for 41 years. "Asa did what was right in the eyes of the Lord, as his father David had done. He expelled the male cult prostitutes from the land and got rid of all the idols his fathers had made. He even deposed his grandmother Maacah from her position as queen mother, because she had made an Asherah pole. Asa cut the pole down and burned it in the Kidron Valley. Although he did not remove the high places, Asa's heart was fully committed *[shalem]* to the Lord all his life" (1 Kings 15:11-14).

Scripture regards Asa as a great reformer. His will to root out every vestige of idolatry in the kingdom was evident. He did not hesitate even to remove his grandmother from office, so strong was his need to please God. Even though the account contains a "but," showing that the reform did not quite fulfill his goal, the accolade is plain: "Asa did that which was right in the eyes of the Lord. . . . Asa's heart was perfect with the Lord all his days" (verses 11-14).

This by no means shows that Asa's life was faultless— far from it. Second Chronicles tells of an occurrence during which the king completely lost confidence in God. Not only did he disregard the message sent to him, but he also imprisoned God's messenger (2 Chron. 16:1-10).

The idea of perfection depicted here is relative. It can comprise intended perfection and desire to act for good and truth that does not always achieve its goal. Thus it can even lack something without causing the person involved to lose the praiseworthy title of "perfect man," which one Scripture attributes to Asa as describing "all his days" (1 Kings 15:14).

Conclusion

Having examined these few examples of individuals that the Old Testament called "perfect," it is now possible to specify the meaning it gave to this word. First of all we need to note that perfection is not confined to a few privileged persons, as the scarcity of examples quoted might at first suggest. On the contrary, it stands out in several other references that God always expected perfection of the congregation of Israel. After the exodus from Egypt, Moses exhorted all the people to be perfect: "Thou shalt be perfect *[tâmîm]* with the Lord thy God" (Deut. 18:13, KJV). Likewise Solomon urged those at the dedication of the Temple: "Let your heart therefore be perfect *[shalem]* with the Lord our God" (1 Kings 8:61, KJV).

It is important, therefore, to emphasize that Scripture never describes perfection as consisting of a sinless nature. Those it calls "perfect" were by no means saints, free from weaknesses, as if they had finally conquered or eradicated the power of sin from their carnal nature. On the contrary, in every case, these "perfect" people continued their struggle against temptations and the tendency to evil within them. Nevertheless, even when there was a failure, their perfection manifested itself in the sincerity of their repentance and in the integrity of their renewed relationship with God.

We should also observe that these "perfect" individuals were people who "walked" with God and in His presence. The qualifying adjective "perfect" appears each time associated with the verb "to walk." The meaning of perfection therefore does not describe a natural state, but a manner of life in close relationship with God, and in a frame of mind that includes such characteristics as sincerity, uprightness, integrity, as well as all the other spiritual characteristics translators have thought necessary to capture the nuances contained in the original Hebrew words *tâmîm* and *shalem*. For as it is written: "The Lord detests men of perverse heart but he delights in those whose ways are blameless *[tâmîm]*" (Prov. 11:20).

Also notice that Scripture likewise places the "walk" of the "perfect" in connection with the ways of the Eternal, that is to say, with His law and His commandments as expressions of His will. This is what God desires from His people: "And now, O Israel, what does the Lord your God ask of you but to fear the Lord your God, *to walk in all his ways,* to love him, to serve the Lord your God with all your heart and with all your soul, and to observe the Lord's commands and decrees that I am giving you today for your own good?" (Deut. 10:12, 13).

Here is a vital truth reiterated repeatedly throughout the Old Testament: life is only possible by observing the physical and moral laws established by the Creator. Human happiness directly depends on them. "Blessed are they whose ways are blameless *[tâmîm;* KJV, "perfect"), *who walk* according to the law of the Lord. Blessed are they who keep his statutes . . . *they walk in his ways*" (Ps. 119:1-3).

It would be wrong to believe, however, that perfection,

according to the teaching of the Old Testament, is the fruit of obedience to God's commandments. The opposite is true. Solomon's prayer at the dedication of the Temple clearly indicates that "to live by His [God's] decrees and obey his commands" it is first necessary that "your hearts must be fully committed [shalem] to the Lord" (1 Kings 8:61).

God also promises all who worship Him: "For the eyes of the Lord run to and fro throughout the whole earth, to shew himself strong in the behalf of them whose heart is perfect [shalem] toward him" (2 Chron. 16:9, KJV). No one has better expressed it than David when he implores God to create in him "a pure heart," to renew in him a "steadfast spirit," and to grant him His "Holy Spirit" in order to "teach transgressors Your ways" (Ps. 51:10-13).

Here are the main lessons that we can draw from the teaching of the Old Testament on the subject of perfection, a goal that God desires every believer to reach.

CHAPTER FOUR

THE CALL OF JESUS TO PERFECTION

As we have just established, perfection, according to the Old Testament, consists essentially of living in close relationship with God, of being in harmony with "the first and greatest commandment": "Thou shalt love the Lord thy God with all thy heart, and with all thy soul, and with all thy mind" (Matt. 22:37, 38, KJV). The teachings of the New Testament, by contrast, put the greater emphasis on the second commandment which "is like unto it, Thou shalt love thy neighbor as thyself" (verse 39, KJV)." On these two commandments," Jesus said, "hang all the law and the prophets" (verse 40, KJV).

That is clearly what emerges from Jesus' teaching on the subject of perfection. In the four gospels the word "perfect" (*téleios*) appears only three times—and only in Matthew's gospel. There it describes relationships with God and humanity. Jesus Himself uses this expression in two very specific circumstances. And each time He does, it is in direct connection with the commandments intended to govern relationships between human beings.

1. "Be ye therefore perfect, even as your Father which is in heaven is perfect"

Jesus uttered this declaration at the conclusion of His comments on the law (Matt. 5:48, KJV). After having affirmed the perpetuity of the law, Jesus systematically contrasted a legalistic observance of the commandments with the perfect obedience of the new spirit that should characterize all who partake of the new covenant.

The issue for Jesus did not consist of knowing whether the law must be observed or not, but rather how we should put it into practice and the motivation behind it, unlike the scribes and Pharisees, who focused on the outward act itself. For "except your righteousness shall exceed the righteousness of the scribes and Pharisees," Jesus declared solemnly, "ye shall in no case enter into the kingdom of heaven" (verse 20, KJV). What Jesus condemned in them, the most religious of their time, was not their zeal in observing God's commandments, but of doing so in a legalistic manner, and of sticking to the letter of the law only, leaving aside "the weightier matters of the law, judgment, mercy, and faith" (Matt. 23:23).

These are exactly the virtues that Jesus expounds in His comments on the law. They constitute the spirit of the law, giving it life, whereas, according to Paul, the letter of the law kills (2 Cor. 3:6). Two examples will suffice to clarify this point.

The first concerns the sixth commandment: "Ye have

heard that it was said by them of old time, Thou shalt not kill; . . . but I say unto you, That whosoever is angry with his brother without a cause shall be in danger of the judgment" (Matt. 5:21, 22, KJV).

The second example involves the seventh commandment: "Ye have heard that it was said by them of old time, Thou shalt not commit adultery; but I say unto you, That whosoever looketh on a woman to lust after her hath committed adultery with her already in his heart" (verses 27, 28, KJV).

The contrast is obvious. Contrary to the common belief among Christians, the Lawgiver of the new covenant does not expect less than He did in the old covenant. Actually He requires much more. He carries His expectations to a much higher level. Not only does He condemn the act, but also and above all the secret thoughts of the heart that led to it, the deep and hidden motives, the very essence of a person itself rather than any outward appearance. As Jesus explains it elsewhere: "For from within, out of the heart of men, proceed evil thoughts, adulteries, fornications, murders, thefts, covetousness, wickedness, deceit, lasciviousness, an evil eye, blasphemy, pride, foolishness: all these evil things come from within, and defile the man" (Mark 7:21-23, KJV).

Having revealed the righteousness contained in the law and the faithfulness required in its observance, Jesus next emphasizes mercifulness. He did so by recalling the commandment that rightly demands from a person perfection of his or her relationship with a neighbor. "Ye have heard that it hath been said, Thou shalt love thy neighbor, and hate thine enemy. But I say unto you, Love your enemies, bless them that curse you, do good to them that hate you, and pray for them which despitefully use you, and persecute you; that ye may be the children of your Father which is in heaven: for he maketh his sun to rise on the evil and on the good, and sendeth rain on the just and on the unjust. For if ye love them which love you, what reward have ye? Do not even the publicans the same? And if ye salute your brethren only, what do ye more than others? Do not even the publicans so? *Be ye therefore perfect, even as your Father which is in heaven is perfect"* (Matt. 5:43-48, KJV).

Placed in its proper context, this ultimate exhortation leaves no room for doubt. God's perfection at issue here, to which He invites all Christians to participate, does not concern the nature of God but His mode of action toward humanity. "God is love" (1 John 4:16). "God is no respecter of persons" (Acts 10:34, KJV). He displays mercy toward the wicked as well as the good. It is what Jesus asks of His disciples as He concludes His comments on the law.

In his Gospel Luke shows in particular God's merciful aspects. When he records Jesus' exhortation, Luke does not write as did Matthew "be perfect," but "be merciful, just as your Father is merciful" (Luke 6:36). Although using two different words in reporting the same statement of Jesus, Matthew and Luke by no means contradict each other. Each expresses faithfully the Master's thought. The two writers merely translate, by two different words, the word shalem that Jesus most likely used. Matthew used *téleios* ("perfect"), while Luke employed *oiktirmon* ("merciful"). Thus, by selecting the word "merciful" rather than the word "perfect," Luke clearly reveals what we must understand about the kind of perfection that Jesus taught.

The perfection to which Jesus invites all his disciples, can only be realized by a loving relationship to our neighbor. This in fact should be the goal of every Christian in

39

order to be perfect. The reason Jesus gives when He urges us to act like God Himself, is that we "may be sons of your father in heaven" (Matt. 5:45). What is so unusual in loving those who love us? Do not the non-Christians do the same? "Be perfect, therefore," in other words, "merciful, just as your Father is merciful."

Faced with this authoritative command, the unavoidable question arises: to what extent is it possible to reach such a level of perfection? Jesus answers this question in his interview with the rich young ruler longing for the assurance of eternal life.

2. "If thou wilt be perfect"

Jesus made this proposal to a man described in the Gospels as "young," "rich," and a "ruler" in Israel (Matt. 19:16-26; Mark 10:17-27; Luke 18:18-27). What more could he have wanted out of life? However, the rich, young, and influential man was not entirely content with himself. He felt a "lack" of something. In fact, that was his last question to Jesus: "What do I still lack?" (Matt.19:20).

Having seen Jesus bless the children, he approached Him with the hope that He would answer his spiritual yearning. "Teacher, what good thing must I do to get eternal life?" Jesus replied: "Why do you ask me about what is good? . . . There is only One who is good" (verses 16, 17).

Christ came right to the point. "No one is good—except God alone" (Mark 10:18). Human beings have nothing in themselves capable of obtaining eternal life. "With man this is impossible" (Matt. 19:26). But Jesus shows the way: "If you want to enter life, obey the commandments" (verse 17).

After all, Christ only recalls here the elementary principle for everything that has life. Life is possible only within the framework of the laws that govern nature at all levels, physical as well as spiritual. In the beginning obedience to the laws of creation was the condition for eternal life. Because the first couple did not respect God's laws, "sin entered the world . . . and death through sin, and in this way death came to all men" (Rom. 5:12).

On another occasion Jesus replied in the same manner to a lawyer (Luke 10:25-27). Near the end of His ministry He repeated this universal principle: "I know that his [the Father's] command leads to eternal life" (John 12:50). Here again, Jesus' concern is not whether we should observe God's commandments. It was to help people understand what they must do to keep them.

Wishing to be specific regarding the commandments that should assure him of eternal life, the young man requested a clarification: "Which ones?" (Matt. 19:18). What a surprising question from a ruler of Israel! Did he want to discover if the Master wished to change the law as others had accused Him of doing? Or did he hope that Jesus would lessen what he had to fulfill? Whatever the young man's intention may have been, Jesus replied with simplicity: "You know the commandments" (Mark 10:19). To remove all misunderstanding, Jesus quoted the rules that govern human relationships: "Do not murder, do not commit adultery, do not steal, do not give false testimony, honor your father and mother." Then to sensitize his questioner toward the positive aspect of the law, Jesus added: "And 'love your neighbor as yourself'" (Matt. 19:18, 19).

The rich young ruler, who had a high opinion of his own righteousness, instantly replied, "Teacher, . . . all these I have kept since I was a boy" (Mark 10:20). Undoubtedly, like many of his generation, he considered himself without fault in his observance of the law. The apostle Paul, before his conversion, considered himself "blameless" toward the righteousness of the law (Phil. 3:6, KJV). But when he came to know Christ, he now understood the spirit of "obedience which leads to righteousness" (Rom. 6:16).

The perfection to which Jesus invites humanity is far more than legalistic obedience. It is more than all the "do nots" of the commands in the Decalogue. To Jesus, perfection is infinitely more than simple abstinence from evil. For "anyone, then, who knows the good he ought to do and doesn't do it, sins" (James 4:17). Therefore He asks that evil be overcome by good, according to the golden rule: "So in everything, do to others what you would have them do to you, for this sums up the Law and the Prophets" (Matt. 7:12).

Before we continue our discussion, however, we need to note in Mark's Gospel this significant detail: "Jesus looked at him and loved him" (Mark 10:21). Better than anyone else, Jesus knew that only a look of sympathy and love could open the heart and change the spirit to a humble attitude. That compassionate look had no other design than to lead the young man to examine himself and to impress upon him the realization that he still lacked something.

The impact of the Master's affection prompted the rich young ruler to raise one last question: "What do I still lack?" (Matt. 19:20). "You still lack one thing," Jesus replied (Luke 18:22). Then He immediately added, "If you want to be *perfect,* go, sell your possessions and give to the poor, and you will have treasure in heaven. Then come, follow me" (Matt. 19:21).

If the rich young ruler really wanted to make up what he lacked and become "perfect," the only way he could overcome his selfishness was by showing mercy toward his neighbors. "If you *want* to be perfect . . ." The religion of Christ is, above all, the religion of freedom. God can only intervene to the extent that we desire to be perfect. Jesus intended His command for the young man to sell his possessions as a means of removing the obstacles that prevented him from coming to and following Jesus.

Not willing to comply with the conditions Jesus had laid down, the young man "went away sad, because he had great wealth" (Matt. 19:22). Then Jesus explained to His disciples that it was difficult for a rich person to enter God's kingdom. In reality, as He specified, it is not riches in themselves that constitute the obstacle, but the "trust" that we place in our wealth (Mark 10:24). Anything in a person's life that assumes more value than Christ becomes a hindrance to following Him, for He alone can lead us to perfection.

What Jesus wanted His disciples to understand was that by themselves they could not attain perfection. "It is easier for a camel to go through the eye of a needle than for a rich man [namely, one who puts his trust in riches] to enter the kingdom of God" (Matt. 19:24). Astonished by Jesus' statement, the disciples asked, "Who then can be saved?" (Verse 25). In view of their amazement and the importance of the question, Jesus again paused in silence. Then, looking at His disciples, He solemnly said to them, "With man this is impossible, but with God all things are possible" (verse 26).

Conclusion

Jesus leaves no doubt that human beings have no power in themselves to obtain eternal life. He had replied to the young man's first question, "No one is good—except God alone" (Mark 10:17); "There is only One who is good"

(Matt. 19:17). As Jesus categorically states, although it is truly necessary to keep the commandments to enter into life, it is no less true that we are incapable of keeping them by ourselves. The only way to life eternal is: first, to *want* to become perfect; then to *deny* ourselves, *come* to Jesus, and *follow* Him.

It is important to note that according to Jesus, perfection is not a static state, but a dynamic of love. The progression of the verbs used in his declaration proves it completely: "If you want to be perfect, *go, sell* your possessions and *give* to the poor. . . . Then *come, follow* me" (verse 21).

Jesus says that it alone is the route that we must follow to pursue perfection. And it is only possible by maintaining a close relationship with Him, or more specifically, by the living of *His* life. "No branch can bear fruit by itself; it must remain in the vine. Neither can you bear fruit unless you remain in me. . . . Apart from me you can do nothing" (John 15:4, 5). For those who remain united with Him, the impossible becomes possible.

CHAPTER FIVE

Perfection According to the Apostle Paul

O f the apostles, Paul is the one who has written most on the subject of perfection. In his view it pertains to all Christians, but never as an absolute notion. On the contrary, Paul essentially presents perfection as a relative idea that applies to each step in "the perfecting of the saints" (Eph. 4:12; KJV). A detailed study of Paul's epistles reveals at least three well-defined steps in perfecting the believer's spiritual life. Because he speaks of "perfecting," it suggests that we should understand perfection as a progressive development and not as an achievement completed once and for all in this life.

1. The perfect or born-again person

Several times Paul uses the word "perfect" *(téleios)* to describe newly converted believers. For example, he writes to the Corinthians that "we speak wisdom among them that are perfect *[téleios]*" (1 Cor. 2:6, KJV). "Spiritual things" can only be comprehended by those who have received "the Spirit of God" and who "have the mind of Christ." "He that is spiritual judgeth all things" (verses 13-16, KJV). Actually, Paul regrets the fact that he was unable to speak to the Corinthians as "spiritual" people, for they were still "mere infants in Christ." "I gave you milk, not solid food, for you were not yet ready for it," he wrote. "Indeed, you are still not ready. You are still worldly. . . . There is jealousy and quarreling among you" (1 Cor. 3:1-3).

Similarly, in writing to the believers in the Philippian church, Paul calls them "perfect" *(téleios)* (Phil. 3:15, KJV), although some of them "on some point . . . think differently" from him (verse 15). So it is possible to be "perfect" without yet having attained the fullness of the knowledge of Christ.

It could even be that those differences of opinion involved perfection itself. Greek philosophy of the time considered perfection in the absolute meaning of the word. Thus perfection was the privilege of gods alone. Could it be that certain Philippian Christians thought they had attained perfection from the fact that since their conversion they actually partook of Christ's divine nature?

Be that as it may, Paul clarifies the issue by relating his own experience: "Not that I have already obtained all this, or have already been made perfect" (verse 12). For him absolute perfection was yet to come. That is why he said: "I press on toward the goal to win the prize for which God has called me heavenward in Christ Jesus" (verse 14). "God will make clear to you," he adds, any point of difference (verse 15). "Only let us live up to what we have already attained. Join with others in following my example" (verses 16, 17). Paul is "confident of this, that he who began a good work in you will carry it on to completion until the day of Christ Jesus" (Phil. 1:6).

Paul could not have said more clearly that he believed absolute perfection still lay in his future and that it would be truly achieved only in the day of the glorious appearing of the Lord Jesus Christ. But until that day, all those who had heard the good news of the gospel and are running the "Christian race" are in his words "perfect." Having made a covenant with the Lord by baptism, they have received the Holy Spirit, through whom they have been begotten into the new life in Christ.

Now Paul carefully explains that "if anyone is in Christ, he is a new creation; the old has gone, the new has come! All this is from God, who reconciled us to himself through Christ" (2 Cor. 5:17, 18).

In his meeting with Nicodemus Jesus had already emphasized the importance of this first step in the Christian life. "No one can see the kingdom of God unless he is born again" (John 3:3). Then He made it even more specific. "No one can enter the kingdom of God unless he is born of water and the Spirit" (verse 5). Finally, for the sake of everyone desiring to undertake the journey to perfection, Jesus said: "You must be born again" (verse 7).

Taking up the same thought again, Paul reiterates this basic truth with even more intensity: "Neither circumcision nor uncircumcision [that is to say, whether a Christian is from Jewish or pagan origin] means anything; what counts is to become a new creation" (Gal. 6:15). Here is what makes an infant in Christ a "perfect" person in the first stage of his or her spiritual development. Paul advises that it is not sufficient just to be born into a new life in

Christ—one must also grow in order to become a mature and complete Christian.

2. The perfect, or sanctified, person

If in a primary sense any person who has accepted Christ as his Saviour is counted as "perfect" by Paul, it is because the righteousness of Christ has covered that individual's sins. Such a person has been justified and in that sense is "perfect." But the idea of perfection is not confined to the theological concept of justification—it implies a progressive sanctification extending throughout life. "Though outwardly we are wasting away, yet inwardly we are being renewed day by day" (2 Cor. 4:16). Paul calls this slow process of the transformation of "the inner man" a "metamorphosis" (see Rom. 12:2). Under the action of the Holy Spirit a converted individual is literally "transformed into his likeness with ever-increasing glory which comes from the Lord who is the Spirit" (2 Cor. 3:18).

With that in mind Paul continues to encourage his readers "to walk and to please God . . . more and more" (1 Thess. 4:1, KJV). He rejoices to note that the faith of the Thessalonians "is growing more and more, and the love every one of you has for each other is increasing" (2 Thess. 1:3). To the "perfect" in Philippi he writes: "This is my prayer: that your love may abound more and more in knowledge and depth of insight, so that you may be able to discern what is best" (Phil. 1:9, 10). And to the Corinthians he states: "Stop thinking like children. In regard to evil be infants, but in your thinking be adults [téleioi]" (1 Cor. 14:20)—that is to say, perfect, complete, mature, adult. Concluding his second epistle to the Corinthians, he wrote: "Our prayer is for your perfection." Then he repeated: "Aim for perfection" (2 Cor. 13:9, 11).

The concept of development, of maturing and Christian growth, appears in a passage from Hebrews, in which Paul said he would like to have given his readers "solid food" (Heb. 5:12). "For every one that useth milk is unskilful in the word of righteousness: for he is a babe. But strong meat belongeth to them that are of *full age [téleion]*, even those who by reason of use have their senses exercised to discern both good and evil. Therefore leaving the principles of the doctrine of Christ, let us go on unto *perfection [teleiósteta]*" (Heb. 5:13-6:1, KJV).

The perfection to which he refers in this context can only be achieved by going beyond "the elementary truths of God's word" (Heb. 5:12). They include "repentance from acts that lead to death, and of faith in God, instruction about baptisms, the laying on of hands, the resurrection of the dead, and eternal judgment" (Heb. 6:1, 2). In other words, the issue in this new phase involves learning to live "the truth that is in Jesus" (Eph. 4:21).

It is necessary that all "those who have once been enlightened, who have tasted the heavenly gift, who have shared in the Holy Spirit, who have tasted the goodness of the word of God and the powers of the coming age" (Heb. 6:4, 5) fulfill the goal of the Christian life, which is nothing less than to "become mature *[téleion]* [KJV, "perfect man"], attaining to the whole measure of the fullness of Christ" (Eph. 4:13). For as Paul explained to the Christians of Ephesus: "You were taught . . . to put off your old self . . . ; to be made new in the attitude of your minds; and to put on the new self, created to be like God in true righteousness and holiness" (verses 22-24).

What Paul explained so clearly to others, he also lived out in his own life. His theology was the fruit of his personal experience with Christ. Unlike the Pharisees that

Jesus denounced, who "say, and do not" (Matt. 23:3, KJV), what the apostle taught, he first lived. Paul is the perfect example of a person transformed by God's grace. At the close of his life, he, who was "once a blasphemer and a persecutor and a violent man" "the worst of sinners" (1 Tim. 1:13, 16), could write to Timothy: "You, however, know all about my teaching, my way of life, my purpose, faith, patience, love, endurance, persecutions, sufferings" (2 Tim. 3:10).

This metamorphosis, as Paul rightly calls it (see Rom. 12:2; 2 Cor. 3:18), illustrates in a concrete way what is truly the perfection of the complete person, the sanctified Christian, who has attained maturity. It is nothing less than the perfection of character. What God's grace achieved for Paul, God desires to accomplish in all Christians. Paul reckons "that in me . . . Christ Jesus might display his unlimited patience as an example for those who would believe on him and receive eternal life" (1 Tim. 1:16).

Several times Paul painted the picture of the individual before and after conversion: the "carnal" man in contrast to the "spiritual" man (1 Cor. 3:1, KJV). For example, he wrote to Titus: "At one time we too were foolish, disobedient, deceived and enslaved by all kinds of passions and pleasures. We lived in malice and envy, being hated and hating one another. But when the kindness and love of God our Savior appeared, he saved us. . . . He saved us through the washing of rebirth and renewal by the Holy Spirit . . . so that, having been justified by his grace, we might become heirs having the hope of eternal life" (Titus 3:3-7).

In the epistle to the Galatians Paul contrasts even more distinctly "the works of the flesh" (Gal. 5:19, KJV) with the fruit of the Spirit. He describes the Christian virtues that constitute perfection of character in the sanctified believer:

"love, joy, peace, patience, kindness, goodness, faithfulness, gentleness and self-control" (Gal. 5:22, 23). Then he adds: "Against such things there is no law" (verse 23).

Each of the virtues expresses the spirit in which Christ's disciples should obey God's commandments. And each describes in a marvelous way a Christian's relationship with his or her neighbor. "If it is showing *mercy,* let him do *it cheerfully"* (Rom. 12:8). "As far as it depends on you, live at *peace* with everyone" (verse 18). "Be *patient* with everyone" (1 Thess. 5:14). "Let your *gentleness* be evident to all" (Phil. 4:5). "And over all these virtues put on *love,* which binds them all together in perfect unity" (Col. 3:14). Paul considered such perfection of character as "the mystery that has been kept hidden for ages and generations, but is now disclosed to the saints," "which is Christ in you, the hope of glory. We proclaim him, admonishing and teaching everyone with all wisdom, so that we may present everyone *perfect [téleios]* in Christ" (Col. 1:26-28).

Does it mean that this perfection of character to which every Christian should advance throughout his life constitutes the omega of the "perfecting of the saints" (Eph. 4:12, KJV). Certainly not! In all his Epistles Paul clearly permits us to catch a glimpse of a further step. "Something better," more perfect still (Heb. 11:40). To know "Christ in us" is still the only "hope of glory" (Col. 1:27).

3. *Perfection is the hope of glory*

Even when we receive the grace in this life to succeed in perfection of character, we still yearn for the glorious perfection promised to the "perfect" in the day of Jesus Christ's advent. For the more we progress on the road to sanctification, the more we are aware of still having imperfection in ourselves as we compare ourselves to the glorious perfection of the resurrected Christ.

At the conclusion of his hymn of love Paul does not fail to remind us that for the present "we know in part and we prophesy in part, but when *perfection [téleion]* comes, the imperfect disappears. . . . Now we see but a poor reflection as in a mirror; then we shall see face to face. Now I know in part; then I shall know fully, even as I am fully known" (1 Cor. 13:9-12).

As long as we live in this mortal body, subject to "the law of sin and death" (Rom. 8:2, KJV), we shall experience only a relative perfection. Like Paul, we must live in the expectation of being able "to be clothed with our heavenly dwelling, so that what is mortal may be swallowed up by life" (2 Cor. 5:2-4). It will happen at the resurrection. "For the perishable must clothe itself with the imperishable, and the mortal with immortality" (1 Cor. 15:53).

Only then will the perfection, of which the apostle had spoken to the "perfect" ones in the Philippian church and to which Paul himself had not yet arrived be attained. Most certainly he had that in mind when he declared: "Not that I have already obtained all this, or have already *been made perfect [teteleiomai]*, but I press on to take hold of that for which Christ Jesus took hold of me. Brothers, I do not consider myself yet to have taken hold of it. But one thing I do: Forgetting what is behind and straining toward what is ahead, I press on toward the goal to win the prize for which God has called me heavenward in Christ Jesus" (Phil. 3:12-14).

The epistle to the Hebrews clearly shows the transition from present perfection to that more perfect perfection. Referring to "the spirits of righteous men made *perfect*" (Heb. 12:23) in this life, he specifies that "these were all commended for their faith, yet none of them received what had been promised. God had planned something better for us so that only together with us would they be made perfect" (Heb. 11:39, 40).

Together, the "perfect" ones of all times will cross the finish line toward the glorious perfection of the risen Christ. Therefore, Paul invites Christians to wait for the day of the Lord, Jesus Christ's coming, a day in which He, "by the power that enables him to bring everything under his control, will transform our lowly bodies so that they will be like his glorious body" (Phil. 3:21).

Conclusion

We can see that the Pauline idea of perfection is extremely rich in its meaning—not that there exist several kinds of perfection, but that the word perfection encompasses various shades of meaning.

The Greek philosophers gave the word perfection an absolute meaning, one that still often dominates the minds of many Christians today. On the contrary, Paul gave the idea of perfection a relative meaning. He never presented perfection as a state of human nature, or as a fixed state of being that everyone would achieve once and for all. Quite the opposite, Paul always saw perfection as the result of the dynamics of love. The power of the Spirit of God impels the believer to walk progressively onward, his or her eyes fixed on the perfect model in Christ.

For this reason, Paul considered as "perfect" anyone who had accepted Jesus as Saviour, whatever his or her level of spiritual experience. God shows no partiality. Knowing what each individual is capable of, He also gives talents to "each according to his ability" (Matt. 25:15). Likewise, the Lord distributes the gifts of the Spirit "to each one, just as he determines" (1 Cor. 12:11). "But to each one of us grace has been given as Christ apportioned it" (Eph. 4:7). Perfection does not depend on the number of talents received, but on the way we increase. This is where each person can find perfection, whatever the level reached in the development of his or her character or personality.

The Pauline concept of perfection includes the idea of perfection without limit. As we have already said, just as God has put into the human heart the thought of "eternity" (Eccl. 3:11), even though we cannot reach it by ourselves, so also has God created in us *an innate need for perfection* that even eternity will be unable to exhaust.

CHAPTER SIX

PERFECTION ACCORDING TO THE APOSTLE JOHN

Some 30 years after Paul's death the apostle John also expressed himself on the subject of perfection in his First Epistle. He identifies the problem of perfection in the context of the idea of sin, obedience to God's commandments, and the love through which perfection finds expression. What John writes does not differ from what Paul taught, but he presents it from a different point of view.

In effect John confirms what has been said throughout this study—that perfection by no means signifies a life free from mistakes, without fault or sin. All those individuals whom the sacred writings call "perfect," have never pretended to have attained a life free from sin. Nowhere do we find it written that they had reached a stage of perfection implying a final victory over their sinful nature. Such a claim is possible only on the basis of a false concept of the nature of mankind and the nature of sin.

1. An important distinction

To understand John's teaching, we must first grasp the difference between *sin* and *sins*. *Sin* describes the *power of sin* that makes human beings *"slaves to sin"* (Rom. 6:17). Speaking of this power, Paul says, "It is *sin* living in me," and "it [works] in the members of my body, waging war against the law of my mind and making me a prisoner of the law of sin at work within my members" (Rom. 7:17, 23). It is this power that impels humanity to sin and to commit sinful acts. Certainly, these acts, which we call *sins,* are the result of the power that dominates humanity's nature. By the grace of God and the Spirit of life that is in Jesus Christ, it is possible to resist the temptations that lead us to commit sins. But the power of sin, inborn in human nature, will remain in humanity as long as we live in "this body of death" (verse 24).

Because they have not distinguished between sin and *sins,* between *the power of sin* and *sinful deeds,* many sincere believers have deceived themselves about the real meaning of perfection, and have often been led astray into a "perfectionism" contrary to biblical teaching. Certainly we cannot understand Christian perfection without considering its relation to the idea of sin. Almost all the references we have considered have placed perfection in direct relationship to God's law. It would therefore be inconceivable that the idea of perfection, on the part of the "perfect" ones, does not imply a life of victory over their faults, their shortcomings with regard to God and their neighbor—in brief, over their sins. In fact, the apostle John is clear on this point, but we have often improperly interpreted what he has said.

2. Does perfection mean a sinless life?

Many Christians lean on certain statements of the apostle John to affirm that perfection requires a sinless life. First, John clearly defines what he understands by sin: "Everyone who sins breaks the law; in fact, sin is lawlessness. But you know that He appeared so that he might take away our sins. And in Him is no sin" (1 John 3:4, 5). Hence, the apostle concludes: "Whosoever abideth in him *sinneth not*: whosoever sinneth hath not seen him, neither known him" (verse 6, KJV).

Then John explains why this is so. "No one who is born of God *will continue to sin*, because God's seed remains in him; *he cannot go on sinning*, because he has been born of God. This is how we know who the children of God are" (verses 9, 10). He adds: "We know that anyone born of God *does not continue to sin;* the one who was born of God keeps him safe, and the evil one cannot harm him" (1 John 5:18).

After citing these forthright passages we can understand why some people think that the Bible demands a perfection that excludes all possibility of sin. But they forget that the same Epistle has other statements that seem to say just the opposite. Thus, for example: "If we claim to be without sin, we deceive ourselves and the truth is not in us. . . . If we claim we have not sinned, we make him out to be a liar and his word has no place in our lives" (1 John 1:8-10). But John adds also: "I write this to you so that you will not sin. But if anybody does sin, we have one who speaks to the Father in our defense—Jesus Christ, the Righteous One" (1 John 2:1).

While such statements can seem contradictory, they

really are not. The apostle John simply makes a distinction between humanity's sinful nature and the attitude of the child of God toward sin. The apostle emphasizes that *no one* is without sin, not even himself, since he includes himself in his own statement. To think otherwise means that "the truth is not in us" (1 John 1:8). Furthermore, by such an attitude we deceive ourselves and make God a liar. Paul reminded us that "Jews and Gentiles alike are all under sin. . . . 'There is no one righteous, not even one'" (Rom. 3:9, 10).

In those passages in which the apostle John considers the Christian's attitude when faced with sin, he states that "he does not sin," that "he does not practice sinning," and that "he cannot sin" (1 John 3:9). Actually, if we consider the form of the Greek verbs, it should be said that he who is "born of God" "does not continue to sin," "no longer practices sin," and "no longer desires to sin," because he no longer lives in rebellion against God. In other words, the Christian who has been reborn no longer has the desire to sin, because "God's seed remains in him" (verse 9). The same power that has made us new creatures also enables us to live in harmony with the will of God expressed in His holy commandments.

As we can see, these passages focus on Christians' attitude toward sin. Having experienced the new birth, their thoughts, desires, and characters have been transformed. Now that they are born of God, believers now hate sin, where before they loved it. Now they love the virtues that they once detested. And they no longer wish to be slaves to sin, since Christ gives them the power to free themselves from it.

In spite of their new attitude toward sin, if anyone born of God happens, in a moment of weakness or by mistake or ignorance, to commit an act contrary to God's will, he or she will not be lost. Saddened, such individuals will hasten to confess their sin and entrust it to Christ, who "is faithful and just and will forgive us our sins and purify us from all unrighteousness" (1 John 1:9). For as John assures us: "If any man sin, we have an advocate with the Father, Jesus Christ the righteous" (1 John 2:1, KJV).

3. The sin that does not lead to death

Again John makes a distinction between what he calls "a sin that leads to death" and "a sin that does not lead to death" (1 John 5:16). It does not mean that there exist two *kinds* of sins. According to John, "all wrongdoing is sin," that is to say, all transgression of the law "is sin" (verse 17). There are, according to him, two possible *attitudes of the sinner toward God:* one of rebellion that results in death and another of repentance, leading to life.

The rebel toward God lives in a state of continual transgression of God's law. But the attitude of the repentant is the mindset of a person who has been reconciled with God and in whom God dwells. Even when he or she transgresses one of God's commandments, this "sin does not lead to death," because it is confessed and pardoned. Also that is why God gives life to the repentant; likewise: "God will give him life. I refer to those whose sin does not lead to death" (verse 16).

The distinction that John thus recognized between the attitude of the Christian who no longer wanted to sin and the reality of a sinless life, Paul also makes between the relative perfection of the "perfect" ones and the absolute perfection that is yet to come. Just as it is for perfection, so is it also for absolute victory over sin. The perfection to which God calls all Christians in this world implies daily victory over willful sins. But as long as we are in "this body of death," we shall remain potential sinners (Rom. 7:24). To claim more is to ignore the truth, thus deceiving ourselves and making God "a liar" (1 John 1:10).

4. *Perfection in love*

The fact that he or she is a sinner should not prevent the Christian from reaching toward perfection. According to John, we can achieve this only through love for God and neighbor, and in obedience to the holy commandments.

Twice John declares in his Epistles that "God is love" (1 John 4:8, 16). "This is how God showed his love among us: He sent his one and only Son into the world that we might live through him. This is love: not that we loved God, but that he loved us and sent his Son as an atoning sacrifice for our sins" (verses 9, 10).

Our love for God therefore finds its source in *His* love. "We love because he first loved us" (verse 19). Therefore, "since God so loved us, we also ought to love one another" (verse 11). "In this way, love is made complete (KJV, "perfect") among us . . . because in this world we are like him" (verse 17). Just as God loves us, we must also love others. For "he has given us this command: Whoever loves God must also love his brother" (verse 21).

For John, brotherly love is truly the sign of Christian perfection. It is the preeminent proof that one "is born of God and knows God" (verse 7). For "if anyone says, 'I love God,' yet hates his brother, he is a liar. For anyone who does not love his brother, whom he has seen, cannot love God, whom he has not seen" (verse 20). But "if we love one another, God dwelleth in us, and his love is *perfected* in us" (verse 12, KJV).

Love is *perfect* only as it demonstrates itself in deeds

and in obedience to the commandments both toward God *and* to our neighbor. John explains: "This is how we know that we love the children of God: by loving God and carrying out his commands. . . . And his commands are not burdensome, for everyone born of God overcomes the world" (1 John 5:2-4).

This truth was so essential for John that he thought it necessary to repeat it several times. "We know that we have come to know him if we obey his commands. The man who says, 'I know him,' but does not do what he commands is a liar, and the truth is not in him. But if anyone obeys his word, God's love is truly made complete in him. This is how we know we are in him" (1 John 2:3-5).

Conclusion

We refer to the apostle John as the disciple of love not only because he was the disciple whom Jesus "loved" (John 19:26; 20:2; 21:7), but also because he made the love of God as manifested in Jesus Christ, the essential theme of his writings. Just as God's perfection reveals itself in His mercy toward humanity, so our perfection should demonstrate itself in love for God and neighbor. "Whoever claims to live in Him must walk as Jesus did" (1 John 2:6).

For John, as for Jesus and for Paul, love is the preeminent visible sign of perfection. It is defined above all else by the way we show that love and the way in which we keep the commandments. For without love "I am nothing," no matter what other Christian virtues I may possess. Paul adds: "If I give all I possess to the poor and surrender my body to the flames, but have not love, I gain nothing" (1 Cor. 13:2, 3).

Love is truly "the bond of perfectness" (Col. 3:14, KJV).

Those who want to be perfect must become "merciful, just as your Father is merciful" (Luke 6:36), in all their relationships with humanity. Here is the goal toward which all the biblical examples that we have just analyzed invite us. What remains to be considered is the divine agencies that God has put at our disposal for attaining Christian perfection.

CHAPTER SEVEN

DIVINE AGENCIES AIDING PERFECTION

H aving defined perfection and having studied it in its various aspects, one important question remains: How does God make possible what is impossible for human beings? What are the divine agencies at our disposal to achieve perfection, "to win the prize for which God has called me heavenward in Christ Jesus" (Phil. 3:14)?

It would be inconceivable that God would have so clearly indicated the goal of the Christian life without providing the practical means for attaining it. Through careful thought we can discover at least three ways, each intended to lead us to Jesus Christ, without whom perfection is not possible. They include the Scriptures, God's law, and the Holy Spirit.

Although these agencies act simultaneously and in perfect harmony, we must study them one at a time.

1. The witness of the Scriptures

For our purposes here, we shall only consider the Word of God's role in connection with the "perfecting of the saints" (Eph. 4:12, KJV). Without the Bible no one could know anything whatever about God or Jesus Christ. "Now this is eternal life: that they may know you, the only true God, and Jesus Christ, whom you have sent" (John 17:3).

The Scriptures in their entirety have as a central theme the person and work of Jesus Christ. When the Jewish leadership asked Him for proof of His Messiahship, He replied: "You diligently study the Scriptures because you think that by them you possess eternal life. These are the Scriptures that testify about me" (John 5:39).

On the road to Emmaus Jesus demonstrated this fact to two of His disciples. "And beginning with Moses and all the Prophets, he explained to them what was said in all the Scriptures concerning himself" (Luke 24:27). Then when He appeared to all of them, He repeated it again: "'This is what I told you while I was still with you: Everything must be fulfilled that is written about me in the Law of Moses, the Prophets and the Psalms.' Then he opened their minds so they could understand the Scriptures" (Luke 24:44, 45).

The Scriptures are more than a mere source of information. For those who receive them as the Word of God, they become a power for sanctification. Christ explained this to those who believed in His Word, when He revealed Himself to them as the Messiah. "Jesus said, 'If you hold to my teaching, you really are my disciples. Then you will know the truth, and the truth will set you free'" (John 8:31, 32). In saying that, Jesus not only showed the condition to fulfill in order to be one of His disciples—to believe and remain in His word—but also the role of the Word in the life of His disciples. Scripture would make known divine truth and its power to liberate.

In several of His parables Jesus compared the power of the Word of God to that of seed sown on the ground. "Night and day, whether he [the sower] sleeps or gets up, the seed sprouts and grows, though he does not know how. All by itself the soil produces corn—first the stalk, then the head, then the full grain in the head" (Mark 4:27, 28). Thus it is for "the man who hears the word and understands it. He produces a crop" (Matt. 13:23).

Having had such an experience in his own life, Paul declares to the Christians in Rome: "I am not ashamed of the gospel, because it is the power of God for the salvation of everyone who believes. . . . For in the gospel a righteousness from God is revealed" (Rom. 1:16, 17).

Speaking of this mysterious power of the Scriptures, the apostle writes in his Epistle to the Hebrews: "For the word of God is living and active. Sharper than any double-edged sword, it penetrates even to dividing soul and spirit, joints and marrow; it judges the thoughts and attitudes of the heart" (Heb. 4:12). In other words, God's Word penetrates to the very depth of the being, laying bare hidden feelings and the most secret thoughts.

The Scriptures therefore constitute the divine agency that God uses as one means of speaking to humanity and of leading them to Jesus, who alone can transform them to His likeness. That is precisely why the gospel must "be preached in the whole world as a testimony to all nations" (Matt. 24:14). For as Paul wrote to his disciple Timothy: "All Scripture is God-breathed and is useful for teaching, rebuking, correcting and training in righteousness, so that the man of God may be thoroughly equipped for every good work" (2 Tim. 3:16, 17). It is impossible to define any better the role of Scripture in the slow process of growth and spiritual development that advances the Christian from one level of perfection to another.

2. The teaching role of the law

The second divine agency God places at our disposal to lead us to Christian perfection is His law. It is the central core of the Scriptures around which hangs the complete revelation of God. "Inscribed by the finger of God" (Ex. 31:18; 32:16) on two tables of stone, the Ten Commandments express both God's character and His desires for humanity.

Unfortunately, a serious misunderstanding exists concerning the law's role in salvation. For centuries many believed in salvation by the works of the law. Today, however, many hold the opposite error, equally dangerous, that faith in Jesus releases the believer from obeying divine law altogether. Both errors completely contradict the teaching of Jesus and His apostles, who never questioned whether it was necessary to keep the law, but under what conditions and in what manner it was possible to obey it.

Obviously, God did not give the law as a means of salvation. "For if a law had been given that could impart life, then righteousness would certainly have come by the law" (Gal. 3:21). Furthermore, "if righteousness could be gained through the law, Christ died for nothing!" (Gal. 2:21). It is not that the law is imperfect. On the contrary, Paul affirms that "the law is holy, and the commandment is holy, righteous and good" (Rom. 7:12). But the law is not, in itself, capable of giving life or even merely maintaining it. More emphatically, it is absolutely impossible for the law to liberate humanity from the slavery of sin, because it was "powerless," being "weakened by the sinful nature" (Rom. 8:3). That is the reason obedience even to divine law could not bring salvation.

No one fought the belief in salvation by the deeds of the law more than Paul. It does not mean that the great apostle denied the importance of obedience to the law, as some tend to claim. On the contrary, Paul writes: "Keeping God's commands is what counts" (1 Cor. 7:19). He recognized that we have been "created in Christ Jesus to do good works, which God prepared in advance for us to do" (Eph. 2:10). In other words, we are not saved "by works," but for "good works," what Paul specifies as the fruit of God's grace (verses 8-10).

Thus, no one can explain the teaching role of the law in the process of salvation by grace through faith better than Paul. He defined this role in these terms: "The law was our schoolmaster to bring us unto Christ" (Gal. 3:24, KJV). Paul applies this principle not only to the moral law but also the ceremonial laws. The Levitical service in the sanctuary had the same objective as it sought to prepare believers in the old covenant for the coming of the Messiah. The sanctuary service foreshadowed the work of salvation that Jesus Christ would accomplish as the Lamb of God predestined to take away the world's sin.

Writing to Christians who had come out of Judaism, the author of the epistle to the Hebrews took great care to show how the law, under the old covenant, led believers to Christ and through Him to perfection. For he wrote, "If *perfection* could have been attained through the Levitical priesthood" (Heb. 7:11), God would not have needed to appoint another high priest in the person of "the Son, who has been made *perfect* forever" (verse 28). Because the sacrifices and offerings presented continually under the old covenant "could not make him that did the service *perfect*" (Heb. 9:9, KJV) or "make perfect those who draw near to worship" (Heb. 10:1), God "by one sacrifice . . . has made *perfect* forever those who are being made holy" (verse 14).

Since the law under the old covenant "made nothing *perfect,*" God therefore introduced "a better covenant" (Heb. 7:19, 22), of which Christ is the mediator. Thanks to His mediation, the law is not something merely written on tables of stone, but will be found even in the believer's heart, according to the promise made to the prophets Jeremiah and Ezekiel: "This is the covenant I will make with them after that time, says the Lord. I will put my laws in their hearts, and I will write them on their minds" (Heb. 10:16; 8:10).

The Lord could not have foretold more clearly the change that would take place in the role of the law thanks to the work of Jesus. Henceforth the law was to play its part as teacher more effectively in order to lead people to Christ. For "through the law we become conscious of sin" (Rom. 3:20; 7:7). In fact, "the man who looks intently into the *perfect* law that gives freedom" (James 1:25) will see himself as he really is.

Without the law we would have no knowledge of sin, and as a result, no need of a Saviour or of grace. But with the sense of guilt it triggers, the law also gives birth to the desire for deliverance. In this way the law serves as a teacher to lead to Christ, so that by faith in Him, we may be "justified freely by his grace" (Rom. 3:24; Eph. 2:8).

The law has yet another role to fill—that of enabling us to know God's will. Being the expression of God's character, the law is also inevitably the demonstration of His righteousness, His love, and His perfection. Because it is "holy, and just, and good" (Rom. 7:12), the law contains the moral and spiritual principles that human beings must have to be able to discern "what God's will is—his good, pleasing and *perfect* will" (Rom. 12:2).

Certainly, by ourselves we are unable to keep God's commandments. Jesus said that "with men it is impossible." And Paul told us why: "The law is spiritual; but I am unspiritual, sold as a slave to sin. . . . I have the desire to do what is good, but I cannot carry it out" (Rom. 7:14-18). By faith in Jesus Christ, God gives us His grace, not to free us from obedience to His commandments, but to liberate us from sin and make us able to do His will, "for it is God who works in you to will and to act according to his good purpose" (Phil. 2:13).

Therefore the law leads the sinner to Christ like a servant to his master, and Christ takes him or her back—repentant, pardoned, and reconciled to keeping God's commandments. Far from having abrogated the law, God's new covenant in Jesus Christ most definitely confirms it. What has been changed, however, is the relationship between human beings and the law. Thanks to Jesus Christ, the law is no longer merely external to us, engraved "on tablets of stone," but "on tablets of human hearts," "written not with ink but with the Spirit of the living God" (2 Cor. 3:3).

3. The work of the Holy Spirit

Without the Spirit of God, which is also the Spirit of Christ, neither the Scriptures nor the law of God can play a decisive role in the Christian's walk to perfection. Both are agencies of perfection only through the influence of the Spirit. "Men spoke from God as they were carried along by the Holy Spirit" (2 Peter 1:21). We need the same Spirit who inspired the Scriptures to help us understand the truths they contain. In the same way, the law, without the Spirit, cannot awaken the conscience, nor can we obey God's commandments without the power of the Spirit "that is at work within us" (Eph. 3:20).

It is true that the nature of the Holy Spirit is a mystery that God has not revealed to us. Jesus was content just to say that the Spirit is "the Counselor . . . , the Spirit of truth who goes out from the Father" (John 15:26). On the other hand, He defined clearly the role that the Spirit plays in salvation, first in His own life, then in the lives of those who would believe in Him throughout the centuries.

Jesus entered our world 2,000 years ago to reconcile humanity to God through the ministry of Christ and the Holy Spirit of whom He was the bearer. Born by the Spirit, anointed by the Spirit at His baptism, Jesus was led by the Spirit, who lived in Him fully. The apostle Paul went as far as to say that "He appeared in a body, was vindicated by the Spirit" (1 Tim. 3:16). Without the Spirit, Jesus could not have successfully accomplished the work of salvation that God had sent Him into the world for.

Several times Jesus spoke of "the Spirit, whom those who believed in him were later to receive." And the evangelist explains that "up to that time the Spirit had not been given, since Jesus had not yet been glorified" (John 7:39). That is why, after having announced His departure, Jesus reassured His disciples by saying to them: "But I tell you the truth: It is for your good that I am going away. Unless I go away, the Counselor will not come to you; but if I go, I will send him to you. When he comes, he will convict the world of guilt in regard to sin and righteousness and judgment" (John 16:7, 8).

Through these words Jesus Himself defined the

Spirit's role both in the lives of His disciples and in all mankind. "But when he, the Spirit of truth, comes, he will guide you into all truth" (John 16:13). "The Holy Spirit, whom the Father will send in my name, will teach you all things and will remind you of everything I have said to you" (John 14:26).

Soon after His resurrection Jesus renewed the promise made on the eve of His departure: "In a few days you will be baptized with the Holy Spirit" (Acts 1:5). Then, repeating it again, He added: "But you will receive power when the Holy Spirit comes on you; and you will be my witnesses in Jerusalem, and in all Judea and Samaria, and to the ends of the earth" (verse 8).

What Jesus promised to the 12 apostles and then fulfilled at Pentecost, He also makes to all who respond to the promptings of the Holy Spirit. Even after His ascension, Christ continually seeks to draw people to Him (John 12:32), to reveal the treasures of the Scriptures, and to make them able, by the Spirit, to "walk as Jesus did" (1 John 2:6).

The Spirit of God has always been available since Pentecost. From that time forward God has given His Spirit to those who ask (Luke 11:13). The Spirit dwells in those who receive this gift, and through the Spirit Christ also dwells in them. Just as God was incarnated in Jesus Christ by the Spirit, so by the Spirit Christ comes to dwell in all who receive Him. Thus, by His ministry Jesus opened the way for the Spirit and gave birth to a new race of people born again by the Spirit.

The apostle Paul, in particular, emphasizes the role of the Spirit in the "perfecting of the saints" (Eph. 4:12, KJV). He declares that "if anyone does not have the Spirit of Christ, he does not belong to Christ" (Rom. 8:9). "No one can say, 'Jesus is Lord,' except by the Holy Spirit" (1 Cor. 12:3). But if the Spirit dwells in us, "the Spirit himself testifies with our spirit that we are God's children" (Rom. 8:16).

Contrary to what some think, the Spirit of God is not the privilege of just a few. To the believers in the church of Corinth, Paul declares: "For we are all baptized by one Spirit into one body . . . and we were all given the one Spirit to drink" (1 Cor. 12:13). Therefore through Christ "we both have access to the Father by one Spirit" (Eph. 2:18).

Wishing to be even still more precise about the Spirit's role in humanity, Paul explains that "through Christ Jesus the law of the spirit of life set me free from the law of sin and death. . . . And so he condemned sin in sinful man, in order that the righteous requirements of the law might be fully met in us" (Rom. 8:2-4). In other words, God gives us the Spirit that we might be able to "walk in the Spirit," step by step, in fulfilling God's will (Gal. 5:25, KJV).

Conclusion

The gift of the Spirit of God is therefore the essential divine power for all aspects of the spiritual life. First, God's Spirit enables us to understand the vital truths found in the Scriptures. Such truths can become "the power of God unto salvation to everyone that believeth" (Rom. 1:16, KJV) only through the influence of the Holy Spirit. In the same way, the law of God can enlighten the conscience only as the Spirit works in the human heart in order "to bring us unto Christ" (Gal. 3:24, KJV).

Only then is the believer "transformed by the renewing of [their] mind, that [they] may prove what is that good, and acceptable, and *perfect,* will of God" (Rom. 12:2, KJV). By responding to the invitation of the Spirit they receive "the right to children of God" (John 1:12), enabling them "to walk" no longer "after the flesh, but after the Spirit" (Rom. 8:4, KJV).

Without the Spirit, nobody can claim to be a disciple of Christ. The Spirit is both the source of our new life in Christ and the condition of our inner transformation to the image of the perfection that is in Christ. Perfection is only possible by the Spirit of God, as He acts with power through the Scriptures and the justice of His law, in the heart of those who, by faith, receive the Lord Jesus Christ.

In summary, Christian perfection is above all the divine call for each of us to live "the truth that is in Jesus" (Eph. 4:21) in all humility and in love for God and for our neighbors. It occurs in response to the invitation of Jesus: "Be ye therefore perfect, even as your Father which is in heaven is perfect" (Matt. 5:48, KJV).

Perfection
of Christian Character

ELLEN G. WHITE COMMENTS

CHAPTER EIGHT

ELLEN G. WHITE AND CHRISTIAN PERFECTION

Among the authors who have dealt with the subject of Christian perfection, no one, to my knowledge, has done it with such faithfulness to the spirit of the Bible and with profound spiritual knowledge as Ellen G. White (1827-1915). A prolific author, her literary work stretched over some 70 years of her active life. At the time of her death her writings included 24 books in circulation already translated into many languages; two others in the process of publication; 5,000 articles printed in various periodicals; about 200 pamphlets on different subjects; and thousands of pages of manuscript. Since her death in 1915 approximately 50 works have appeared in the form of compilations from her writings.

1. A work centered on Jesus Christ

The Scriptures served as the primary inspiration for all the subjects she dealt with in her writings. For her, the Bible alone served as the criterion of truth. She made a spiritual commentary on it in four large volumes. Then a fifth volume focused on the struggle between the forces of good and evil during the two millennia of Christianity. But the person of Jesus Christ constitutes her preferred theme. Ellen White devoted several works to Him, the most important being *The Desire Ages,* and the most extensively circulated, the volume *Steps to Christ.* The latter has been translated into more than 120 languages. *Thoughts From the Mount of Blessing* and *Christ's Object Lessons* also covered the teachings of Jesus. She wrote on almost everything that touches the Christian's spiritual life, including such subjects as health and education.

Strange as it may seem, not a single one of her books directly concerns Christian perfection or the perfection of Christian character. Yet it is a concept present throughout all her writings. The words "perfection" and "perfect" appear thousands of times from her inspired pen, and the expressions "perfection of character" and "Christian perfection" occur well into the hundreds. For this reason it is not possible here to consider her treatment of the subject in complete detail. It will suffice to make a synopsis, employing the author's own expressions as much as possible.

Because Ellen White believed in perfection, she strove to teach it in all her writings. Repeatedly she invited her readers to aim toward perfection with their whole person through God's grace. For her, perfection was not only a gift of God and a privilege for everyone, but also the marvelous possibility of unlimited spiritual development by following Jesus' model of perfect spiritual stature. "The

78

greatest manifestation of [the Spirit's] power is seen in human nature brought to the perfection of the character of Christ" (7T 143).

2. A completely relative perfection

It is essential to begin our study by trying to define the specific meaning that Ellen White generally gives to the word perfection. In spite of certain expressions that seem absolute, some of which people have used to draw wrong conclusions from, she presents Christian perfection as an essentially relative concept.

Certainly, many passages invite us to a perfection that appears to be the very perfection of God Himself. Others seem to affirm that our perfection must be equal to that of Christ, our model. Just as Jesus invites us to be "perfect . . . as your heavenly Father" (Matt. 5:48), so Ellen White writes that "the ideal of Christian character is Christlikeness" (8T 64). "As the Son of man was perfect in His life, so His followers are to be perfect in their life" (DA 311). "God requires perfection of His children" (COL 315).

Nevertheless, a careful reading leaves no doubt concerning the relative nature of perfection in Ellen White's mind. "All righteous attributes of character dwell in God as a perfect, harmonious whole" (COL 330). But, as we shall see, human beings do not have all of them nor have them in the same way.

Even though we are "privileged to possess these attributes" *(ibid.)* by imitating our perfect and divine Example, we will never be more than a reflection of His image. "We cannot equal the pattern; but we shall not be approved of God if we do not copy it and, according to the ability which God has given, resemble it" (2T 549). In fact, God asks each of us to do only that which we are able. "He places every human agent under obligation to do his best. Moral perfection is required of all" (COL 330).

In Ellen White's mind Christ's invitation to become "perfect . . . as your heavenly Father is perfect" was clearly relative. Several times she repeated the following comment: "As God is perfect in His sphere, so man may be perfect in his sphere" (MM 112-113; 8T 64; 4T 591; PP 574). Notice that she sees these "spheres" as distinguishable from each other. Furthermore, she even seems to adapt moral perfection to the particular nature of each individual. "With our limited powers we are to be as holy in our sphere as God is holy in His sphere. To the extent of our ability, we are to make manifest the truth and love and excellence of the divine character. As wax takes the impression of the seal, so the soul is to take the impression of the Spirit of God and retain the image of Christ" (1SM 337).

Thus the notion of perfection takes on many shades of meaning. First, Ellen White discerns different degrees of perfection in all that God created. "Perfection exists in the least as well as in the greatest of the works of God" (Ed 114). Different individuals have different levels of perfection. "Not all reach the same development or do with equal efficiency the same work. God does not expect the hyssop to attain the proportions of the cedar, or the olive the height of the stately palm. But each should aim just as high as the union of human with divine power makes it possible for him to reach" (ibid. 267). Even more important, a person can continuously be at the level of perfection during the development of his or her spiritual life. Just as a plant is perfect at every level of its growth, so "at every stage of development our life may be perfect" (ibid. 106; COL 65).

The perfection that the believer can attain is relative for yet another reason—our imperfect sinful nature. Not only is perfection of the flesh impossible, but moral perfection itself is limited by our way of life before conversion, and by the continuing physical, intellectual, and moral effects of that past life. So Ellen White speaks of people whose sins God has forgiven, but who still carry the scars, the marks, and the effects of these sins for the rest of their lives (3BC 1153; 5T 41).

However relative our moral perfection may be, "those who would be workers together with God must strive for perfection of every organ of the body and quality of the mind" (COL 330). For "while we cannot claim perfection of the flesh, we may have Christian perfection of the soul" (2SM 32). It is required of every follower of Christ. Here again, a precise understanding is imperative: Christian perfection of the soul is relative to the action of God. "Our dependence is not in what man can do; it is in what God can do for man through Christ" *(ibid.)*.

Ultimately, the moral perfection to which Ellen White constantly refers is clearly described by the expression "the perfection of the character" that we find time and again in her books.

3. *The perfection of Christian character*

"The Lord requires perfection from His redeemed family. He calls for perfection in character-building" (5BC 1085). It is a clearly defined perfection that is nothing less than an explicit demand. "God will accept only those who are determined to aim high. He places every human agent under obligation to do his best. Moral perfection is required of all. Never should we lower the standard of righteousness in order to accommodate inherited or cultivated tendencies to wrongdoing. We need to understand that imperfection of character is sin" (COL 330).

According to Ellen White, the development of character "determines destiny, both for this life and for the life to come" (Ed 109). It is both "the harvest of life" *(ibid.)* and the "passport . . . to the higher grade, the school above" *(ibid.* 19). There is nothing more important than the formation of character, and nothing is of greater price in the eyes of God. "The choicest productions of human skill possess no beauty that can bear comparison with that beauty of character which in His sight is of 'great price'" *(ibid.* 249). Jesus also devoted the better part of His teaching to character building. "He said nothing to gratify curiosity or to stimulate selfish ambition. He did not deal in abstract theories, but in that which is essential to the development of character; that which will enlarge man's capacity for knowing God, and increase his power to do good" *(ibid.* 81).

For some time we have known that "character building is the most important work ever entrusted to human beings; and never before was its diligent study so important as now" *(ibid.* 225). Of course, "true education does not ignore the value of scientific knowledge or literary acquirements; but above information it values power; above power, goodness; above intellectual acquirements, character. The world does not so much need men of great intellect as of noble character" *(ibid.* 225).

"But such a character is not the result of accident; it is not due to special favors or endowments of Providence. A noble character is the result of self-discipline, of the subjection of the lower to the higher nature—the surrender of self for the service of love to God and man" *(ibid.* 57). It also demands patience and perseverance. "Perfection of character is a lifelong work, unattainable by those who are not willing to strive for it in God's appointed way, by slow and toilsome steps. We cannot afford to make any mistake in this matter, but we want day by day to be growing up into Christ, our living Head" (5T 500).

"But Christ has given us no assurance that to attain perfection of character is an easy matter. A noble, all-round character is not inherited. It does not come to us by accident. A noble character is earned by individual effort through the merits and grace of Christ. God gives the talents, the powers of the mind; we form the character. It is formed by hard, stern battles with self. Conflict after conflict must be waged against hereditary tendencies. We shall have to criticize ourselves closely and not allow one unfavorable trait to remain uncorrected" (COL 331).

4. A work of God's grace

However, even if the perfecting of character is to a large extent the result of our personal efforts, it is no less the product of God's grace. In fact, character perfection is the fruit of intimate collaboration between God and human beings. Through Jesus Christ, God gives humanity the power to attain the marvelous ideal of the perfection of Christian character. That is also why the Lord "expects from us the perfection which Christ revealed in His humanity" (CG 477). "In his efforts to reach God's ideal for him, the Christian is to despair of nothing. Moral and spiritual perfection, through the grace and power of Christ, is promised to all" (AA 478). "With the light of truth shining upon us, we cannot now be excused for a moment in meeting a low standard. As coworkers with Christ, we are privileged to share with Christ in His suffering. We are to look at His life, study His character, and copy the pattern.

What Christ was in His perfect humanity, we must be; for we must form characters for eternity" (TM 173).

"We are not yet perfect; but it is our privilege to cut away from the entanglements of self and sin, and advance to perfection. Great possibilities, high and holy attainments, are placed within the reach of all" (AA 565). "There should be continual striving and constant progress onward and upward toward perfection of character" (8T 64). "The kingdom of God comes not with outward show. It comes through the gentleness of the inspiration of His word, through the inward working of His Spirit, the fellowship of the soul with Him who is its life. The greatest manifestation of its power is seen in human nature brought to the perfection of the character of Christ" (7T 143). "No longer are the members of the church to remain unconcerned in regard to the formation of right characters. Placing themselves under the molding influence of the Holy Spirit, they are to form characters that are a reflection of the divine character" (8T 86). "None need fail of attaining, in his sphere, to perfection of character. By the sacrifice of Christ, provision has been made for the believer to receive all things that pertain to life and godliness. God calls upon us to reach the standard of perfection and places before us the example of Christ's character. In His humanity, perfected by a life of constant resistance of evil, the Saviour showed that through cooperation with Divinity, human beings may in this life attain to perfection of character. This is God's assurance to us that we, too, may obtain complete victory" (AA 531).

CHAPTER NINE

PERFECTIBILITY, HUMANITY'S PRIVILEGE

To grasp in their entirety Ellen White's thoughts on the perfection of Christian character, we must observe what she considers to be the essential attribute of human character, namely its perfectibility. In this sense, even less than in its other aspects, perfection does not appear as an absolute, as something finished or as a complete quality bestowed on humanity in the beginning by the Creator, but rather as a possibility for infinite development that even eternity can not exhaust.

Certainly God created humanity perfect, exhibiting in the human race the very perfection that marks everything He brings into existence. But humanity's perfection does differ from that of other creatures, because of the possi-

85

bility for experiencing unlimited progress. Humanity can become ever more than it was before. Such constantly increasing perfectibility is possessed neither by inanimate nature nor by other forms of life. It is the privilege of the only earthly creature made in God's image.

But it also carries with it the risk of sin. God could have created human beings other than in His own image, fashioning them in such a way that our first parents could not have disobeyed Him. "God might have created them without the power to transgress His requirements, *but in that case there could have been no development of character;* their service would not have been voluntary, but forced. Therefore He gave them the power of choice—the power to yield or to withhold obedience" (Ed 23; italics supplied).

That says it all—human perfectibility lies in our potential of unlimited development of character that only a voluntary submission to God's laws renders possible. "A mere forced submission would prevent real development of mind or character; it would make man a mere automaton. Such is not the purpose of the Creator. He desires that man, the crowning work of His creative power, shall reach the highest possible development" (SC 43, 44).

In Eden God created Adam and Eve's world in such a manner as to assure perfectly their physical, mental, and spiritual growth. "Useful occupation was appointed them as a blessing, to strengthen the body, *to expand the mind, and to develop the character*" (Ed 21; italics supplied). If our first parents had faithfully followed God's commands, they would have been "fitted *more and more fully* to reflect, throughout endless ages, the light of the knowledge of His glory" (*ibid.* 22; italics supplied). For God's aim in creating humanity in His image was precisely "that the longer man lived the more fully he should reveal this image—the more fully reflect the glory of the Creator. . . . But by disobedience this was forfeited" (*ibid.* 15).

Indeed, the tempter cunningly made our first parents believe that the Creator "was thus seeking to prevent them from reaching a nobler development and finding greater happiness" (*ibid.* 24). As a result, through disobedience to the divine injunction humanity lost the marvelous privilege that belonged to it: the possibility of endless development, the privilege of going forward from perfection to perfection. For "by the mingling of evil with good, his mind had become confused, his mental and spiritual powers benumbed" (*ibid.* 25). But so that "the divine purpose in [humanity's] creation might be realized," God put into execution the plan of redemption that would permit Him "to restore in man the image of his Maker, *to bring him back to the perfection in which he was created,* to promote the development of body, mind, and soul" (*ibid.* 15, 16; italics supplied).

1. The possibility of unlimited development

"Higher than the highest human thought can reach is God's ideal for His children. Godliness—godlikeness—is the goal to be reached" (*ibid.* 8). However, let no one mistakenly assume that we can reach such a goal in its fullness during this life. God's ideal only opens before us "a path of continual progress" *(ibid.).* Anyone who has received the power to become a child of God had begun a new life. A fundamental characteristic of life is growth. "The development of the plant is a figure of the development of character. There can be no life without growth. The plant must either grow or die. As the growth is silent and imperceptible, but continuous, so is the growth of character. At every stage of development our life may be perfect; yet if God's purpose for us is fulfilled, *there will be constant advancement*" (*ibid.* 105, 106; italics supplied).

Understood in this way, perfection describes both a state gained by the authentic Christian and also a goal to be reached in the future. It was exactly the position of Christ's disciples whom Paul referred to as perfect but who in reality had not reached full perfection. "Even the most perfect Christian may increase continually in the knowledge and love of God," Ellen White explains (1T 340). Because of human perfectibility, "every day we may advance in perfection of Christian character" (GW 274). The possibility of humanity's continual development is not only a privilege but also a real need of human nature. It is so much a requirement of Christian character that Ellen White could not imagine the eternal existence of the redeemed without the possibility of unlimited perfection.

"In eternity we shall learn that which, had we received the enlightenment it was possible to obtain here, would have opened our understanding. The themes of redemption will employ the hearts and minds and tongues of the redeemed through the everlasting ages. They will understand the truths which Christ longed to open to His disciples, but which they did not have faith to grasp. Forever and forever new views of the *perfection and glory of Christ will appear.* Through endless ages will the faithful Householder bring forth from His treasure things new and old" (COL 134; italics supplied).

"Those who give heed to the instructions of the divine Teacher, constantly advance in wisdom, refinement, and nobility of soul, and thus they are prepared to enter that higher school where advancement will continue throughout eternity" (CT 51). "Through ceaseless ages to advance in wisdom, in knowledge, and in holiness, ever exploring new fields of thought, ever finding new wonders and new glories, ever increasing in capacity to know and to enjoy and to love, and knowing that there is still beyond us joy and love and wisdom infinite—such is the object to which the Christian's hope is pointing" (*ibid.* 51, 55).

"And the years of eternity, as they roll, will bring richer and still more glorious revelations of God and of Christ. As knowledge is progressive, so will love, reverence, and happiness increase. The more men learn of God, the greater will be their admiration of His character" (GC 678).

"If it were possible for us to attain to a full understanding of God and His word, there would be for us no further discovery of truth, no greater knowledge, no further development. God would cease to be supreme, *and man would cease to advance.* Thank God, it is not so. Since God is infinite, and in Him are all the treasures of wisdom, we may to all eternity be ever searching, ever learning, yet never exhaust the riches of His wisdom, His goodness, or His power" (Ed 172; italics supplied). "Those who are under the instruction of Christ in this world will take every divine attainment with them to the heavenly mansions. And in heaven we are continually to improve" (MYP 100, 101).

"The exceeding rewards for right-doing, the enjoyment of heaven, the society of the angels, the communion and love of God and His Son, the elevation and extension of all our powers throughout eternal ages—are not these mighty incentives and encouragements to urge us to give the heart's loving service to our Creator and Redeemer?" (SC 21). "Christ in you, the hope of glory" (Col. 1:27). "A knowledge of this mystery furnishes a key to every other. It opens to the soul the treasures of the universe, *the possibilities of infinite development*" (Ed 172; italics supplied).

Ellen White so clearly expresses this idea of the perfectibility of humanity first of all, then of the redeemed, that she therefore excludes all idea of absolute perfection. Absolute perfection exists only in God, and Christ alone is its perfect expression. Our resemblance to our divine Model can only be a likeness continually renewed "as the perfection of His [God's] character is dwelt upon" (*ibid.* 18). If there were an absolute in human perfection, it would have to be sought in the possibility of advancing constantly toward a perfection that could not be surpassed and that would then equal even God's.

All that we can say about human perfection will therefore always and inevitably be relative. Consequently, every time Ellen White uses these expressions we must understand them in the light of this fundamental idea. It is especially true of all that has been said and written about the perfection that the saints of the last generation must attain.

2. Character perfection: the goal of life

Reading Ellen White's writings quickly leads us to conclude that all her ethics hinge on the problem of moral perfection that every Christian must reach if he or she would not render null and void Christ's redemptive sacrifice. Such moral perfection expresses itself in the character. This explains also, the importance she placed upon the perfection of character. By constantly calling our attention to this special aspect of the problem of perfection, Ellen White doubtless wanted to fix our minds on what should concern us most directly.

There are no other perfections possible for a human being before he or she attains perfection of character. This one effects all the others, especially the perfection of the flesh. Without transformation of character, without regeneration of the entire being, we can have no hope of taking part in the resurrection of God's children. No one will be able to see God unless he or she is first sanctified. "When Christ shall come, our vile bodies are to be changed, and made like His glorious body; but the vile character will not be made holy then" (OHC 278). It is in this life that we must effect character perfection.

This explains why Ellen White reiterates time and again her counsels on the subject. Our need to sanctify the entire being, to reach perfection, is a truth that appears on every page of her writings. In a commentary on the Second Epistle of Peter, for example, she shows clearly that the apostle's intention was to set "forth the divine plan for the development of Christian character" (AA 529).

"God has called His people to glory and virtue, and these [attributes] will be manifest in the lives of all who are truly connected with Him. Having become partakers of the heavenly gift, they are to go on unto perfection, being 'kept by the power of God through faith.' It is the glory of God to give His virtue to His children. He desires to see men and women reaching the highest standard; and when by faith they lay hold of the power of Christ, when they plead His unfailing promises, and claim them as their own, when with an importunity that will not be denied they seek for the power of the Holy Spirit, they will be made complete in Him" (AA 530).

The promise of divine help is so sure that "none need fail of attaining, *in his sphere,* to perfection of Christian character. By the sacrifice of Christ, provision has been made for the believer to receive all things that pertain to life and godliness. God calls upon us to reach the standard of perfection, and places before us the example of Christ's character. In His humanity, perfected by a life of constant resistance of evil, the Saviour showed that through cooperation with Divinity, *human beings may in this life attain to perfection of character.* This is God's assurance to us that we, too, may obtain complete victory" (*ibid.* 531; italics supplied).

"Before the believer is held out the wonderful possibility of being like Christ, obedient to all the principles of the law" (*ibid.* 532). Certainly "Satan had claimed that it was impossible for man to obey God's commandments; and in our own strength it is true that we cannot obey them. But Christ came in the form of humanity, and by His perfect obedience He proved that humanity and divinity combined can obey every one of God's precepts. 'As many as received him, to them gave he power to become the sons of God, even to them that believe on his name' (John 1:12, KJV). This power is not in the human agent. It is the power of God. When a soul receives Christ, he receives power to live the life of Christ" (COL 314).

That is why "God requires perfection of His children. His law is a transcript of His own character, and it is the standard of all character. This infinite standard is presented to all that there may be no mistake in regard to the kind of people whom God will have to compose His kingdom. The life of Christ on earth was a perfect expression of God's law, and when those who claim the children of God become Christlike in character, they will be obedient to God's commandments" (*ibid.* 315).

"'Give diligence,' he [Peter] pleaded, 'to make your calling and election sure: for if ye do these things, ye shall never fall: for so an entrance shall be ministered unto you abundantly into the everlasting kingdom of our Lord and Saviour Jesus Christ.' Precious assurance! Glorious is the hope before the believer as he advances by faith towards the heights of Christian perfection!" (AA 533).

3. The perfection of the living at the return of Jesus

Ellen White devotes so much attention to the subject of perfection of character for still another reason. For Christians of the final generation, those who will be alive at Christ's coming, character perfection is even more imperative. "Enoch's life and character, which were so holy that he was translated to heaven without seeing death, represent what the lives and characters of all must be, if, like Enoch, they are to be translated when Christ shall come" (OHC 278).

In *Early Writings* Ellen White solemnly declares: "I saw that none could share the 'refreshing' unless they obtain the victory over every besetment, over pride, selfishness, love of the world, and over every wrong word and action" (EW 71). Inevitably such "a change will be seen in the character, the habits, the pursuits. . . . The character is revealed, not by occasional good deeds and occasional misdeeds, but by the tendency of the habitual words and acts" (SC 57, 58). However, "even one wrong trait of character, one sinful desire, persistently cherished, will eventually neutralize all the power of the gospel" (*ibid.* 34). It is therefore indispensable that we strive for complete victory over every one of our weaknesses.

It is for this purpose that God will send, before He finishes His work on earth and in the human heart, the latter rain intended to ripen the grain for the harvest. This special gift that God will bestow on His children of the last generation will complete the character formation of those who will have taken seriously their preparation for the day of the Lord. "By the power of the Holy Spirit the moral image of God is to be perfected in the character. We are to

93

be wholly transformed into the likeness of Christ. The latter rain, ripening earth's harvest, represents the spiritual grace that prepares the church for the coming of the Son of man" (TM 506).

"Now is the time to prepare. The seal of God will never be placed upon the forehead of an impure man or woman. It will never be placed upon the forehead of the ambitious, world-loving man or woman. It will never be placed upon the forehead of men or women of false tongues or deceitful hearts. All who receive the seal must be without spot before God—candidates for heaven." And "when the decree goes forth and the stamp is impressed, their character will remain pure and spotless for eternity" (5T 216).

Recognizing our duty to reach the Christian ideal, we should ask ourselves the following questions: "Are we striving with all our power to attain to the stature of men and women in Christ? Are we seeking for His fullness, ever pressing toward the mark set before us—the perfection of His character? When the Lord's people reach this mark, they will be sealed in their foreheads. Filled with the Spirit, they will be complete in Christ, and the recording angel will declare, 'It is finished'" (6BC 1118).

The Great Controversy describes this process in detail: "Those who are living upon the earth when the intercession of Christ shall cease in the sanctuary above are to stand in the sight of a holy God without a mediator. Their robes must be spotless, their characters must be purified from sin by the blood of sprinkling. Through the grace of God and their own diligent effort they must be conquerors in the battle with evil. While the investigative judgment is going forward in heaven, while the sins of penitent believers are being removed from the sanctuary, there is to be a special work of purification, of putting away of sin, among

God's people upon earth. . . . When this work shall have been accomplished, the followers of Christ will be ready for His appearing" (GC 425).

"When He [Jesus] comes, He is not to cleanse us of our sins, to remove from us the defects in our characters, or to cure us of the infirmities of our tempers and dispositions. If wrought for us at all, this work will be accomplished before that time. When the Lord comes, those who are holy will be holy still. Those who have preserved their bodies and spirits in holiness, in sanctification and honor, will then receive the finishing touch of immortality. . . . No work will then be done for them to remove their defects and give them holy characters. The Refiner does not then sit to pursue His refining process, and remove their sins and their corruption. This is all to be done in these hours of probation. It is *now* that this world is to be accomplished for us" (2T 355).

"The heavenly character must be acquired on earth, or it can never be acquired at all" (*ibid.* 267). For "death brings dissolution to the body, but makes no change in the character. The coming of Christ does not change our characters; it only fixes them forever beyond all change" (5T 466).

"If you would be a saint in heaven, you must first be a saint on earth. The traits of character you cherish in life will not be changed by death or by the resurrection. You will come up from the grave with the same disposition you manifested in your home and in society. Jesus does not change the character at His coming. The work of transformation must be done now. Our daily lives are determining our destiny" (AH 16).

"Now, while our great High Priest is making the atonement for us, we should seek to become perfect in Christ. Not even by a thought could our Saviour be brought to yield to the power of temptation. Satan finds in human hearts some point where he can gain a foothold; some sinful desire is cherished, by means of which his temptations assert their power. But Christ declared of Himself: 'The prince of this world cometh, and hath nothing in me'" (John 14:30, KJV). Satan could find nothing in the Son of God that would enable him to gain the victory. He had kept His Father's commandments, and there was no sin in Him that Satan could use to his advantage. This is the condition in which those must be found who shall stand in the time of trouble" (GC 623).

4. Who is sufficient for these things?

We could cite many more quotations that exhort us to develop the character. "There should be continual striving and constant progress onward and upward toward perfection of character" (8T 64). Ellen White continually presents the Christian life as a constant journey forward, the goal of which is nothing less than "to form characters that are a reflection of the divine character" (*ibid.* 86). Christians have not always understood this truth, but it is important that those living in the end time should not forget it. For those who will have the privilege of living in the last hours of the world's history without knowing death, character perfection—a perfect sanctified life—will be an absolute necessity. "Nothing but holiness will prepare you for heaven. It is sincere, experimental piety alone that can give you a pure, elevated character and enable you to enter into the presence of God, who dwelleth in light unapproachable" (2T 267). "Blessed are the pure in heart, for they will see God" (Matt. 5:8).

Such a high ideal and such specific requirements make us somewhat dizzy. They may threaten to overwhelm us.

Who is sufficient for these things? Who indeed would dare to attempt to reach for this standard? If we went no further than the simple declaration of the Christian ideal, it would only discourage most people. And it is sure to happen whenever we do not emphasize at the same time and with even greater force the marvelous grace that the Lord wants to give us. Make no mistake that "we have nothing in ourselves of which to boast. We have no grounds for self-exaltation. Our only ground of hope is in the righteousness of Christ imputed to us, and in that wrought by His Spirit working in and through us" (SC 63).

If it is imperative to be clothed with the perfection of Christ's character when we appear before God, it is just as indispensable that we let Christ Himself clothe us with His character, His righteousness, His perfection. He alone can bring to perfection the work that He undertakes in our hearts. If we desire it, "He who began a good work in you will carry it on to completion until the day of Christ Jesus" (Phil. 1:6).

CHAPTER TEN

CHARACTER PERFECTION POSSIBLE ONLY IN JESUS CHRIST

Many have presented the necessity of attaining character perfection in this life as our individual responsibility. We certainly do have to work out our own salvation "with fear and trembling," as the apostle Paul writes, but at the same time we must never forget that "it is God who works in you to will and to act according to his good purpose" (Phil. 2:12,13). "For it is by grace you have been saved, through faith—and this not from yourselves, it is the gift of God" (Eph. 2:8).

Ellen White constantly taught this fundamental truth. Certain quotations taken out of their context could appear to give the impression that she preached salvation by works, and—what would be infinitely more serious—could discourage those faced with the impossibility of achieving this Christian ideal. Others, blinded into thinking they are measuring up to that ideal, could become puffed up with pride and self-righteousness. But she never makes a single reference to character perfection without at the same time showing Jesus Christ as the only means of attaining it. Careful reading of the quotations we have already cited should suffice to prove this, although we will take the liberty of adding a few more.

1. Contemplation of the character of Jesus

"There is no true excellence of character *apart from Him*" (SC 21; italics supplied). Only by contemplating Christ's character can we bring about the desired transformation of our own characters. "As the flower turns to the sun, that the bright beams may aid in perfecting its beauty and symmetry, so should we turn to the Sun of righteousness, that heaven's light may shine upon us, that our character may be developed in the likeness of Christ" (*ibid.* 68). If we model our life after His, "the loveliness of the character of Christ will be seen in [us] His followers" (*ibid.* 59).

The first step toward perfection is therefore a step toward Jesus Christ. "So you are not to look to yourself, not to let the mind dwell upon self, but look to Christ. Let the mind dwell upon His love, upon the beauty, the perfection, of His character. Christ in His self-denial, Christ in His humiliation, Christ in His purity and holiness, Christ in His matchless love—this is the subject for the soul's contemplation. *It is by loving Him, copying Him, depending wholly upon Him, that you are to be transformed into His likeness*" (*ibid.* 70, 71; italics supplied).

It is an absolute requirement. "We should dwell upon the character of our dear Redeemer and Intercessor. . . . As we meditate upon the perfections of the Saviour, we shall desire to be wholly transformed and renewed in the image of His purity. There will be a hungering and thirsting of soul to become like Him whom we adore" (*ibid.* 89). Furthermore, in proportion to our ongoing transformation by the grace of Jesus Christ, so will the soul's admiration for the character of its divine Model ever increase. The Christian, "beholding as in a glass the glory of the Lord, . . . is changed from glory to glory, until he is like Him whom he adores" (AA 559).

So as by a kind of Christian osmosis the character of Jesus Christ forms in us. A transformation similar to that seen in the life of the apostle John becomes possible for each of us. "His resentful, ambitious temper was yielded to the molding power of Christ. The regenerating influence of the Holy Spirit renewed his heart. The power of the love of Christ wrought a transformation of character. *This is the sure result of union with Jesus.* When Christ abides in the heart, the whole nature is transformed" (SC 73; italics supplied).

"There may be marked defects in the character of an individual, yet when he becomes a true disciple of Christ, *the power of divine grace* transforms and sanctifies him" (AA 559; italics supplied). Love for God is powerful, "it modifies the character, governs the impulses, controls the passions, subdues enmity, and ennobles the affections" (SC 59). "Then with Christ working in you, you will manifest the same spirit and do the same good works—works of righteousness, obedience" (*ibid.* 63).

"Through faith, every deficiency of character may be supplied, every defilement cleansed, every fault corrected, every excellence developed" (AA 564). "You are just as dependent upon Christ, in order to live a holy life, as is the branch upon the parent stock for growth and fruitfulness.

. . . It is by communion with Him, daily, hourly—*by abiding in Him*—that we are to grow in grace. He is not only the Author, but the Finisher of our faith" (SC 69; italics supplied). "The life you have received from Me can be preserved only by continual communion. . . . As the vine branch constantly draws the sap from the living vine, so are we to cling to Jesus, and receive from Him by faith the strength and perfection of His own character" (DA 676).

No one therefore should be deceived in his efforts for perfection of character. No holiness can exist apart from Christ, and without the help of the Spirit of God no transformation is possible. We have absolutely nothing in ourselves that we can count on, even after our initial victories. Only an uninterrupted communion with, and continual dependence on God, through Christ and by faith, can enable us to keep what we have gained and at the same time advance ever onward to new heights. "He who is trying to become holy by his own works in keeping the law is *attempting an impossibility*" (SC 60; italics supplied).

Certainly, thanks to Christ's victory and to real cooperation with God, "before the believer is held out the wonderful possibility of being like Christ, obedient to all the principles of the law. *But of himself man is utterly unable to reach this condition.* The holiness that God's word declares he must have before he can be saved is the *result of the working of divine grace* as he bows in submission to the discipline and restraining influences of the Spirit of truth. *Man's obedience can be made perfect only by the incense of Christ's righteousness,* which fills with divine fragrance every act of obedience. The part of the Christian is to persevere in overcoming every fault. Constantly he is to pray to the Saviour to heal the disorders of his sin-sick soul. *He has not the wisdom or the strength to overcome;*

these belong to the Lord, and He bestows them on those who in humiliation and contrition seek Him for help" (AA 532; italics supplied).

2. Perfect, but not without sin

"There are those who attempt to ascend the ladder of Christian progress; but as they advance, they begin to put their trust in the power of man" *(ibid.)*. Such a temptation lies in wait for all who have once experienced the Lord's victorious power. Always we must remember that it is impossible to say at any one moment in his life: "I have fully attained!" "None of the apostles and the prophets ever claimed to be without sin. Men who have lived nearest to God, men who would sacrifice life itself rather than knowingly commit a wrong act, men whom God has honored with divine light and power, have confessed the sinfulness of their nature. They have put no confidence in the flesh, have claimed no righteousness of their own, *but have trusted wholly in the righteousness of Christ.*

"So will it be with all who behold Christ. The nearer we come to Jesus, and the more clearly we discern the purity of His character, the more clearly shall we see the exceeding sinfulness of sin, and the less shall we feel like exalting ourselves. There will be a continual reaching out of the soul after God, a continual, earnest, heartbreaking confession of sin and humbling of the heart before Him. At every advance step in our Christian experience, our repentance will deepen. *We shall know that our sufficiency is in Christ alone* and shall make the apostle's confession our own: 'I know that in me (that is, in my flesh) dwelleth no good thing.' 'God forbid that I should glory, save in the cross of our Lord Jesus Christ, by whom the world is crucified unto me, and I unto the world' (Rom. 7:18, KJV; Gal. 6:14, KJV)" (AA 561; italics supplied).

"The attitude of Paul is the attitude that every follower of Christ should take as he urges his way onward in striving for the immortal crown. Let those who feel inclined to make a high profession of holiness look into the mirror of God's law. As they see its far-reaching claims, and understand its work as a discerner of the thoughts and intents of the heart, they will not boast of sinlessness" (*ibid.* 562).

"And the claim to be without sin is, in itself, evidence that he who makes this claim is far from holy. It is because he has no true conception of the infinite purity and holiness of God or of what they must become who shall be in harmony with His character; because he has no true conception of the purity and exalted loveliness of Jesus, and the malignity and evil of sin, that man can regard himself as holy. The greater the distance between himself and Christ, and the more inadequate his conceptions of the divine character and requirements, the more righteous he appears in his own eyes" (GC 473).

"All who are truly sanctified will have a similar experience [to that of Daniel]. The clearer their views of the greatness, glory, and perfection of Christ, the more vividly will they see their own weakness and imperfection. They will have no disposition to claim a sinless character; that which has appeared right and comely in themselves will, in contrast with Christ's purity and glory, appear only as unworthy and corruptible. It is when men are separated from God, when they have very indistinct views of Christ, that they say 'I am sinless; I am sanctified'" (SL 50).

"There can be no self-exaltation, no boastful claim to freedom from sin, on the part of those who walk in the shadow of Calvary's cross. They feel that it was their sin which caused the agony that broke the heart of the Son of God, and this thought will lead them to self-abasement. Those who live nearest to Jesus discern most clearly the frailty and sinfulness of humanity, and their only hope is in the merit of a crucified and risen Saviour" (GC 471).

The perfection of character of Christ's true disciples will therefore never be a self-sufficient perfection. On the contrary, it will ever be all the more perfect as they increasingly feel their need to depend on the very perfection of Christ, their Saviour. "The more our sense of need drives us to Him and to the Word of God, the more exalted views we shall have of His character, and the more fully we shall reflect His image" (SC 65).

We see this clearly shown in the attitude of those who will live through the time of trouble. Although they have attained perfection of character and the all-powerful grace of the Lord guards them from all sin, "in their whole lives they can see little good. They are fully conscious of their weakness and unworthiness. Satan endeavors to terrify them with the thought that their cases are hopeless, that the stain of their defilement will never be washed away. . . . Though God's people will be surrounded by enemies who are bent on their destruction, yet the anguish which they suffer is not a dread of persecution for the truth's sake; they fear that every sin has not been repented of, and that through some fault in themselves they will fail to realize the fulfillment of the Saviour's promise: I 'will keep thee from the hour of temptation, which shall come upon all the world.' . . . They afflict their souls before God, pointing to their past repentance of their many sins" (GC 619).

"As long as Satan reigns we shall have self to subdue,

besetments to overcome, and there is no stopping place, there is no point to which we can come and say we have fully attained" (1T 340). "We cannot say, 'I am sinless,' till this vile body is changed and fashioned like unto His glorious body" (ST Mar. 23, 1888). In other words, not only will the struggle continue until the very end of the conflict; it will in fact reach its climax during the time of trouble.

However, just as God did not reject Jacob at the brook Jabbok, "God will not cast off those who have been deceived and tempted and betrayed into sin, but who have returned unto Him with true repentance. . . . God's love for His children during the period of their severest trial is as strong and tender as in the days of their sunniest prosperity; but it is needful for them to be placed in the furnace of fire; their earthliness must be consumed, that the image of Christ may be perfectly reflected" (GC 621).

3. Clothed with the righteousness of Christ

So whether it concerns imputed or imparted righteousness, it is always Christ's righteousness that is involved. "If you give yourself to Him, and accept Him as your Saviour, then, sinful as your life may have been, for His sake you are accounted righteous. Christ's character stands in place of your character, and you are accepted before God just as if you had not sinned" (SC 62).

The same process takes place when, by sanctification, God clothes us with a character that resembles more and more that of Jesus. "It is the righteousness of Christ, His own unblemished character, that through faith is imparted to all who receive Him as their personal Saviour" (COL 310). The wedding garment in Christ's parable symbolizes "the pure, spotless character which Christ's true followers will possess" *(ibid.).*

"This robe, woven in the loom of heaven, has in it not one thread of human devising. Christ in His humanity wrought out a perfect character, and this character He offers to impart to us" (*ibid.* 311). "When we submit ourselves to Christ, the heart is united with His heart, the will is merged in His will, the mind becomes one with His mind, the thoughts are brought into captivity to Him; we live His life. This is what it means to be clothed with the garment of His righteousness" (*ibid.* 312).

Certainly the Saviour wants us to be more than repentant sinners. He has provided for all our needs so that we may also become dedicated saints, participating even in this life and in our body of humiliation in the perfecting of a divine character through faith in Christ. Every day we must learn "to choose . . . that royal robe woven in heaven's loom—the 'fine linen, clean and white' (Rev. 19:8, KJV), which all the holy ones of earth will wear. This robe, Christ's own spotless character, is freely offered to every human being. But all who receive it will receive and wear it here" (Ed 249).

"Clothed in the glorious apparel of Christ's righteousness, they have a place at the King's feast. They have a right to join the blood-washed throng" (COL 315). "Only the covering which Christ Himself has provided can make us meet to appear in God's presence. This covering, the robe of His own righteousness, Christ will put upon every repenting, believing soul" (*ibid.* 311).

We can never remind ourselves enough that "we have nothing in ourselves of which to boast. We have no ground for self-exaltation. Our only ground of hope is in the righteousness of Christ imputed to us, and in that wrought by His Spirit working in and through us" (SC 63).

If we constantly strive to follow Jesus, the promised

blessing of standing before the throne of God, "without stain or wrinkle or any other blemish" (Eph 5:27), is ours, attained in Christ as He clothes us with His righteousness and His perfection.